FENDI

YOUR SEVEN WAYS TO ROME

ART, PARKS, RESTAURANTS, SHOPPING, AND MORE FUN

RIZZOLI
NEW YORK

New York Paris London Milan

Thanks to Emanuela Nobile Mino for the texts, Flavia Lazzarini
for the playlists and Flavia Grazioli for the illustrations.

Translation by
Sylvia Adrian Notini

First published in the United States of America in 2017 by
Rizzoli International Publications, Inc.
300 Park Avenue South
New York, NY 10010
www.rizzoliusa.com

Originally published in Italian in 2016 by
Rizzoli Libri S.p.A

2017 2018 2019 2020 / 10 9 8 7 6 5 4 3 2 1

ISBN: 978-0-8478-7893-3289-9

Library of Congress Control Number: 2016945402

Printed in Italy

Table
of Contents

THE MAGIC OF ROME

Seven is the number of the city's hills, like the ancient kings of Rome; seven is the number of the Jubilee churches, but also of the virtues and the cardinal sins. The President of Italy holds office for seven years, and there are also seven days in the week, seven musical notes, seven colors in the rainbow, seven stars in the Big Dipper. And then there are the seven wonders of the ancient and modern world, seven alchemical metals, the Ancient Greeks sailed seven seas; there are seven liberal arts, and seven chakras, and they say you'll have seven years of bad luck if you break a mirror...

In the Eternal City, about which everything has already been said, yet everything is still waiting to be discovered, where past and future go hand in hand, we've found the magic key that opens up all the doors: a handbook to the city divided into seven chapters, with lots of itineraries so you can lose yourself and then find your way again while strolling amid the art and the history. You can visit the seven churches, admire the museums and the private collections, stand in awe before the works by Caravaggio, go looking for the talking statues and the Baroque fountains ... and you can enjoy the best of contemporary Rome and the wonders of its parks and

villas, finishing things off with a visit to see the city's markets and stands.

After walking around all day it's time to unwind, and this handbook will take care of you, suggesting the city's best wellness and beauty centers, the places where you can drink a good glass of wine and taste such culinary delights you'll feel like you're in seventh heaven: the best fish restaurants, traditional Roman ones, cafés and bistros for breakfast or snacks, and the many parks and gardens in the Eternal City where you can plan a picnic. Also included are the most fashionable places to go, where you can experience Rome from dusk to dawn and finish your day on a high note.

For each itinerary we've created a soundtrack, suggested in the playlist at the beginning of each chapter. Each entry, in addition to a description, includes the practical information you'll need, the name of a place nearby where you can stop to eat or just rest, and a curiosity related to the same place.

In the last pages of the book you can take personal notes, scribble down the names of the places you've been, and anything about this wonderful city you think is interesting.

Enjoy your visit!

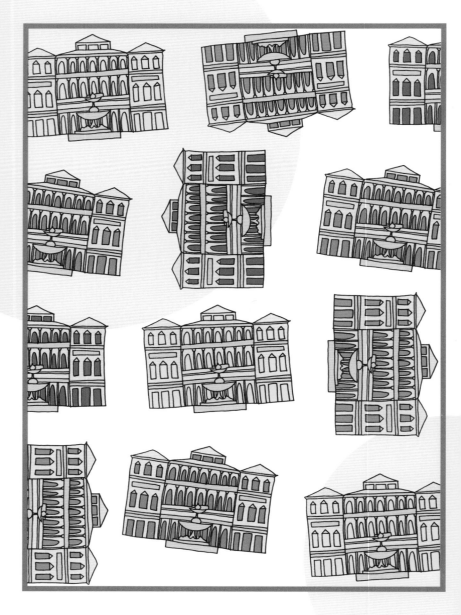

A STROLL THROUGH ART AND HISTORY

. Playlist .

"CHURCH DREAM"
Alva Noto + Ryuichi Sakamoto

"DELILAH"
Florence + The Machine

"KAMALOKA"
GoGo Penguin

"LEVANTE"
President Bongo

"TAKE ME TO CHURCH"
Hozier

"IN A LANDSCAPE"
John Cage

"ALL IS FULL OF LOVE"
Björk

TOURING THE SEVEN CHURCHES

A tour of the seven churches is closely linked to the priest Filippo Neri who, beginning on Jeudi Gras 1552, transformed one of the traditions of the medieval pilgrims into an annual celebration. To encourage the faithful to pray and not give in to the distractions and the "pagan seductions" of the Carnival, Filippo Neri organized a long walk, which was actually more like a day in the country, alternating prayer with leisure activities. During the two days, the pilgrims had to stop at seven of the most important churches in the city, in this order: San Pietro, San Paolo fuori le mura, San Sebastiano fuori le mura, San Giovanni in Laterano, Santa Croce in Gerusalemme, San Lorenzo fuori le mura, and, lastly, Santa Maria Maggiore. Since then, a tour of the seven churches is repeated every year on Jeudi Gras.

San Giovanni in Laterano

The papal Archbasilica of Saint John Lateran is Rome's cathedral and the "mother and head of all the churches of the city and the world." Built by Constantine after the Christians were granted freedom of worship, it represents the true link between the pagan and Christian eras. After Constantine defeated Maxentius in battle, he ordered the huge barracks on the Laterani family's land to be razed and a church built in its place. Consecrated by Pope Sylvester I, this church is where all the popes were elected until the nineteenth century. Francesco Borromini was commissioned to refurbish the church in 1650, marking his first opportunity to work on architecture of monumental dimensions. The facade was added later by Alessandro Galilei in 1732. The bishop's throne is located in the apse and can be reached by walking down the central nave, whose floor is decorated in Cosmatesque style. Located next to the basilica was the patriarchate, also known as the *dimora lateranense*, the seat of the papacy and the pope's official residence until 1309. The pope's private chapel, called Sancta Sanctorum, and the Scala Santa (Holy Staircase) can also be visited.

piazza di San Giovanni in Laterano 4
+39 06 698 86 433
open 7 a.m.-6:30 p.m. (cloister 9 a.m.-6 p.m.)
vicariatusurbis.org

INSIDE THE BAPTISTERY, THE DOORS OF THE CHAPEL DEDICATED TO SAINT JOHN WEIGH OVER 1,500 POUNDS EACH; THEY ARE MADE OF A BRONZE ALLOY COMBINED WITH PRECIOUS METALS, INCLUDING SILVER AND GOLD. THIS WOULD SEEM TO EXPLAIN WHY THE ROTATING HINGES PRODUCE A PARTICULARLY MELODIOUS SOUND, MUCH LIKE THAT OF AN ORGAN.

EATING TIP
DOMENICO DAL 1968
via Satrico 23/25
+39 06 704 94 602
domenicodal1968.it
open 12:30-3 p.m.,
8-11:30 p.m.
Mon 8-11:30 p.m.
closed Sun

 5 MINUTES

SAN LORENZO FUORI LE MURA

What is especially intriguing about Saint Lawrence outside the Walls is its architectural layout, for it is the result of merging two churches—one dated to the late sixth century, the other to the early twelfth century—into one. Both churches were built around the tomb of Saint Lawrence, a Spanish deacon who died a martyr during the persecution of Emperor Valerian. Featured inside the basilica, which also preserves the remains of Saint Stephen, are floors in the Cosmatesque style as well as numerous treasures and splendid mosaics in the apse vault. The twelfth-century cloister is small yet magnificent. The church was bombed during the Second World War, and the subsequent restoration, which took only five years, was unable to bring back the beautiful frescoes that had once decorated the facade.

THE COSMATI WERE A ROMAN FAMILY OF MARBLE WORKERS, ACTIVE BETWEEN THE TWELFTH AND THIRTEENTH CENTURIES, WHO INVENTED A DECORATIVE MOTIF FEATURING LARGE CIRCLES MADE OF POLYCHROME INLAID MARBLE. THE PATTERN WAS WIDELY USED AND THE STYLE CAME TO BE KNOWN AS COSMATESQUE.

piazzale del Verano 3
+ 39 06 491 511
open winter 7:30 a.m.-12:30 p.m.
and 3:30-7 p.m; summer
7:30 a.m.-12:30 p.m. and 4-8 p.m.
vicariatusurbis.org

EATING TIP
PASTIFICIO
SAN LORENZO
via Tiburtina 196
+ 39 06 972 73 519
pastificiosanlorenzo.com
open 12:30 -3 p.m.
and 8-11:30 p.m.
Sat 8-11:30 p.m. closed Sun

 4 MINUTES

SAN PAOLO FUORI LE MURA

With its majestic Byzantine structure, the Papal Basilica of Saint Paul outside the Walls is the second largest church in Rome, after Saint Peter's. The magnificence of the mosaics on the facade greets us in the very place where, legend has it, Paul the apostle is buried. It was Paul who led the way to evangelization and who, not far from here, was martyred in the first century. His tomb, a small church that Emperor Constantine had built and that was consecrated in 324 by Pope Sylvester I, became an important destination for pilgrims, to the point that in 391, under the joint reign of three emperors (Theodosius I, Gratian, and Valentinian II), it was decided that it should be expanded. In 1823 a terrible blaze lasting over five days destroyed most of the basilica; however, the splendid ciborium by Arnolfo di Cambio, a spectacular Gothic tabernacle in porphyry from 1285, was miraculously saved, and the precious mosaics in the church interior and on the facade were later restored. Reconstruction began, thanks to Pope Leo XII, and ended in 1928 with the outer quadriporticus made up of 150 columns.

piazzale di San Paolo 1
+39 06 698 80 800
open 7 a.m.-6:30 p.m.
basilicasanpaolo.org

LOCATED HERE IS A FAMOUS SERIES OF TONDI WITH THE PORTRAITS OF ALL THE POPES, FROM SAINT PETER TO POPE FRANCIS. LEGEND HAS IT THAT ONCE ALL THE TONDI ARE FILLED, JUDGEMENT DAY WILL COME.

EATING TIP
RISTORO
DEGLI ANGELI
via Luigi Orlando 2
+39 06 514 36 020
ristorodegliangeli.it
open 12:30-2:30 p.m.
and 7:30-11:30 p.m.
closed Sun

🚶 10 MINUTES

SAN PIETRO

Saint Peter's is the most important and the largest basilica of the Catholic religion, rising from the burial site of the first apostle of Jesus and first pope of the Catholic church. The ancient basilica of Constantine was originally located here, built under the papacy of Sylvester I, who consecrated it in 326. After a period of abandonment, at the start of the sixteenth century Pope Julius II commissioned Donato Bramante to design the new Vatican basilica and the fabric of Saint Peter as the institution in charge of the works. Saint Peter's is brimming with Italian art and architectural treasures, boasting works by some of the greatest masters of all time: Giuliano da Sangallo, Raphael, Carlo Maderno, creator of the facade. To Michelangelo is due the splendid cupola, and Gian Lorenzo Bernini created the majestic bronze baldachin (canopy) and the oval piazza, encompassing a majestic colonnade of 284 columns and 88 pillars in travertine. It is an act of devotion to touch the right foot of the bronze statue of Saint Peter made by Arnolfo di Cambio: indeed the foot has been worn down by the repeated gesture of the millions of faithful.

piazza San Pietro, Città del Vaticano
+ 39 800 038 436
open 7 a.m.-6:30 p.m. winter;
7 a.m.-7 p.m. summer
vicariatusurbis.org

AT THE BASE OF THE CANOPY'S COLUMNS ARE EIGHT MARBLE FRIEZES, APPARENTLY ALL THE SAME: LEGEND HAS IT THAT THEY REPRESENT THE STAGES FROM PREGNANCY TO BIRTH, PERHAPS IN REFERENCE TO THE "MOTHER CHURCH." THERE ARE ALSO SOME WHO SUGGEST THE ALLUSION IS TO POPE JOAN...

EATING TIP
ASSUNTA MADRE
via Giulia 14
+39 06 688 06 972
assuntamadre.com
open 7 p.m.-midnight

 9 MINUTES

SAN SEBASTIANO FUORI LE MURA

Saint Sebastian outside the Walls rises outside the Mura Aureliane (Aurelian Walls), which closed off the ancient city of Rome; the church is located on the very site where it is said the earthly remains of the apostles Peter and Paul were preserved and venerated during the persecution of Christians. Following the freedom of worship granted by Constantine, the apostles' remains could then be returned to their original sites (Saint Peter's and Saint Paul outside the Walls); the church was subsequently dedicated to Saint Sebastian, the martyr buried here. The Chapel of the Relics contains the relics of many saints, including those of Saints Peter, Paul, Andrew, and Nereus and Achilleus. It also holds the thorns from Jesus's crown, an arrow from Saint Sebastian's martyrdom, and the "Quo vadis" stone, which is said to bear Christ's footprints.

PETER WAS FLEEING PERSECUTION VIA THE APPIAN WAY WHEN JESUS APPEARED BEFORE HIM. "LORD, *QUO VADIS?*" (WHERE ARE YOU GOING), PETER ASKED, AND JESUS ANSWERED: "I AM GOING TO ROME TO BE CRUCIFIED AGAIN." THE APOSTLE UNDERSTOOD THAT HE SHOULD RETURN TO ROME AND ACCEPT HIS MARTYRDOM, AND HE OBEYED.

via Appia Antica 136
+ 39 06 780 88 47
open 8 a.m.-1 p.m. and 2-5:30 p.m.
vicariatusurbis.org
catacombe.org

EATING TIP
APPIA ANTICA CAFFÈ
via Appia Antica 175
+39 06 898 79 575
appiaanticacaffe.it
open March-Oct 8 a.m.-8 p.m; Nov-Feb 8 a.m.-5 p.m.
closed Mon

🚶 12 MINUTES

SANTA CROCE IN GERUSALEMME

Dating from the fourth century, the Basilica of the Holy Cross in Jerusalem houses the important relics brought by Helen, mother of Emperor Constantine, from the Holy Land. These include parts of the True Cross, on which Jesus was crucified, two thorns from the crown, a Holy Nail, and the Titulus Crucis (INRI, the inscription carved on the cross), as well as part of the cross of one of the two thieves. The church is decorated with medieval frescoes, polychrome marble mosaics, and splendid floors in Cosmatesque style. The cycle of frescoes in the apse (1430-1510), of rare beauty, tells the "Story of the True Cross," and is the work of Antoniazzo Romano. Also worth visiting is the adjoining basilica museum, which contains the frescoes that decorated the upper part of the walls of the central nave, as well as some artworks from the fourteenth century.

DOWN A FLIGHT OF STAIRS IS THE BEAUTIFUL CHAPEL OF SAINT HELEN, FEATURING MOSAICS ON THE CEILING. UNTIL 1935, WOMEN COULD ENTER THE CHAPEL ONLY ONCE A YEAR, ON MARCH 20, AS THE CARVING AT THE ENTRANCE INFORMS US, UNDER PENALTY OF EXCOMMUNICATION.

piazza di Santa Croce in Gerusalemme
+ 39 06 706 13 053
open 7 a.m.-12:45 p.m. and 3:30-7:30 p.m.
santacroceroma.it

EATING TIP
OTTAVIO
via di Santa Croce
in Gerusalemme 9
+39 06 702 85 95
ottavio.it
open 8 p.m.-midnight
closed Sun

 2 MINUTES

SANTA MARIA MAGGIORE

This church, the most important of the Roman churches dedicated to the Virgin Mary, was founded by Pope Liberius in 358. Legend has it that on the night of August 5, the pope had a dream in which the Virgin asked him to build a church on the spot where he found fresh snow the next morning. The morning after it snowed on Esquiline Hill, and since then each year on August 5 the Miracle of the Snow is celebrated, during which a spectacular "snowfall" of white petals floats down before the basilica, illuminating and "refreshing" the summer night. Gian Lorenzo Bernini is buried at the high altar under a simple slab of marble. Many popes are also buried in this church, and it contains the world's first manger, made by Arnolfo di Cambio in 1291. The steeple of Santa Maria Maggiore is Rome's tallest, at 246 feet.

SANTA MARIA MAGGIORE IS ALSO KNOWN AS A "*BASILICA AD PRAESEPEM*" FROM THE LATIN *PRAESEPIUM*, OR "FEEDING TROUGH." THE GLASS CABINET UNDER THE HIGH ALTAR CONTAINS A PRECIOUS RELIC BROUGHT FROM THE HOLY LAND: THE FRAGMENTS OF THE MANGER THE CHRIST CHILD WAS PLACED IN WHEN HE WAS BORN.

piazza di Santa Maria Maggiore 42
+39 06 698 86 800
open 7 a.m.-7 p.m.
vicariatusurbis.org

EATING TIP
LA MATRICIANA
via del Viminale 44
+39 06 488 17 75
lamatriciana.it
open 12-3 p.m.
and 7-11 p.m.
closed Sat

 6 MINUTES

Great Museums and Family Collections

Between the sixteenth and eighteenth centuries, feverish archaeological excavations in Rome and the surrounding area unearthed masterpieces that had been buried for centuries. Thanks to the enlightened vision of the great aristocratic and "papal" families like the Borghese, the Ludovisi, the Barberini, and the Doria Pamphilj, who commissioned the leading artists and architects to make works of art and architecture, several private collections of inestimable historical and artistic value took shape in the Eternal City. Today, we can admire these seven collections by entering the residences that have always safeguarded them, preserving these treasures for the benefit of future generations.

. PLAYLIST .

"SUN CITY CREEPS"
Woods

"ROLLER"
Quilt

"LAKE SUPERIOR"
The Arcs

"TBD"
SBTRKT (feat. Sampha)

"WATER ME"
FKA twigs

"FOOTSTEPS"
Rhò

"COOL MELT"
HVOB

Galleria Borghese

The Galleria Borghese's collection of artworks is known as the "queen of all the private collections in the world," owing to the quality and significance of its treasures: sculptures and mosaics from the Roman age appear alongside celebrated works made in the fifteenth through seventeenth centuries by some of the most famous names in art history—Antonello da Messina, Giovanni Bellini, Caravaggio, Gian Lorenzo Bernini, Raphael, Titian, Correggio, Antonio Canova. We owe the original core of the collection to the acquisitions of Cardinal Scipione Borghese in the early seventeenth century, to which were added those inherited from the noblewoman Olimpia Aldobrandini. The layout is still the one requested by Marcantonio IV Borghese (1730–1800): at the center of each room are major masterpieces of ancient sculpture, while the decorations on the walls and ceilings, designed specifically for this purpose, recall the theme represented by the sculptures. Reservations are required to visit the gallery.

PERHAPS THE MOST FAMOUS WORK OF ALL AT THE GALLERIA BORGHESE IS THE STATUE OF PAOLINA BONAPARTE, ANTONIO CANOVA'S MASTERPIECE. RECLINING ON A PILLOWED COUCH IN A SEDUCTIVE POSITION, THE FIGURE OF PAOLINA, NAPOLEON'S SISTER, HAS BECOME AN EMBLEM OF BEAUTY AND SENSUALITY.

piazzale Scipione Borghese 5
+39 06 841 65 42
open 9 a.m.-7 p.m., closed Mon
galleriaborghese.beniculturali.it

EATING TIP
IL GATTO E L'UVA
via Savoia 68
+39 06 855 773
ilgattoeluva.com
open 12-3 p.m.
and 7-11 p.m.
Sat 7-11 p.m.
closed Mon

 11 MINUTES

GALLERIA COLONNA

In 1650 Cardinal Girolamo I Colonna rebuilt the ancient medieval family palazzo, turning it into a sumptuous patrician residence and one of the most beautiful examples of Roman Baroque style. The initial architectural project by Antonio del Grande was added to by Gian Lorenzo Bernini, Paolo Schor, and Carlo Fontana. The splendid frescoed rooms of the gallery host a wealth of masterpieces arranged one next to the other, climbing all the way up to the ceiling, as family collections traditionally do. Among these are works by such masters of Italian painting as Cosmé Tura, Bronzino, Annibale Carracci, Pietro da Cortona, Guercino, Tintoretto, Paolo Veronese. In the early twentieth century, Isabelle, Prince Marcantonio Colonna's Lebanese consort, lived here. Her apartment, which is still intact, is a treasure trove on a par with the great French rooms of Versailles; as well as countless objects, it preserves many refined paintings made by artists of the caliber of Pinturicchio and Pomarancio.

via della Pilotta 17
+39 06 678 43 50
open Sat 9 a.m.-1:15 p.m.
galleriacolonna.it

DID YOU NOTICE? THIS IS THE VERY PLACE HIT BY A CANNONBALL FIRED BY THE FRENCH ARTILLERY FROM THE JANICULUM DURING THE UPRISINGS OF THE ROMAN REPUBLIC IN 1849. THE CANNONBALL LANDED RIGHT ON THE PALAZZO STAIRCASE, SPLITTING THE MARBLE IN HALF.

EATING TIP
ABRUZZI
via del Vaccaro 1
+39 06 679 38 97
open
12:30-3 p.m. and
7-11 p.m.

 3 MINUTES

GALLERIA DORIA PAMPHILJ

This gallery was established in 1651 by Giambattista Pamphilj, who was elected pope under the official name of Innocent X. Situated outside the imposing Palazzo Doria Pamphilj - one of the few in Rome still inhabited by the descendants of the original family, with a vast assemblage of artworks and furnishings that is still intact - the Gallery can boast of one of the largest private collections, enriched over the years through shrewd acquisitions and marriages. Among the most precious works are the famous *Portrait of Innocent X* by Diego Velázquez, the *Rest on the Flight into Egypt* by Caravaggio, the marble bust of Olimpia Maidalchini Pamphilj by Alessandro Algardi, and innumerable works by Guercino, Raphael, Guido Reni, Parmigianino, Titian, Lorenzo Lotto, Filippino Lippi, Gian Lorenzo Bernini, Annibale Carracci, and Pieter Bruegel the Elder, as well as a priceless collection of Flemish paintings.

via del Corso 305
+39 06 679 73 23
open 9 a.m.-7 p.m.
doriapamphilj.it

EATING TIP
ENOTECA CORSI
via del Gesù, 87/88
+39 06 679 08 21
enotecacorsi.com
Mon-Sat 9 a.m.-7 p.m.
Thur and Fri
9 a.m.-midnight
closed Sun

 5 MINUTES

Palazzo Altemps

Now one of the four seats of the Museo Nazionale Romano (the other three are Palazzo Massimo, the Baths of Diocletian, and the Crypta Balbi), the Palazzo Altemps was built by Girolamo Riario in the fifteenth century to a design by Melozzo da Forlì; it was later named after the Austrian cardinal Mark Sittich Altemps, who purchased it in 1568 and took up residence here. Leased as a diplomatic site, it was one of the city's worldliest locations in the eighteenth century. Even Mozart performed here during one of his stays in Rome. The frescoed rooms of Palazzo Altemps host numerous Greek and Roman sculptures collected between the sixteenth and seventeenth centuries by some of Rome's greatest aristocratic families, including the Boncompagni Ludovisi, the Mattei, the Del Drago, and, of course, the Altemps. Of particular interest is the Egyptian collection, which includes many objects found in Egypt and Rome. A great number of them come from a temple devoted to the Egyptian deities Isis and Serapis in Campo Marzio: this is proof of just how widespread the cult of Egypt was in Ancient Rome.

piazza di Sant'Apollinare 46
+39 06 399 67 700
open 9 a.m.-7:45 p.m., closed Mon
archeoroma.beniculturali.it

EATING TIP
LO ZOZZONE
PIZZERIA AL TAGLIO
via del Teatro Pace 32
+39 06 688 08 575
open 10 a.m.-11 p.m.

 5 MINUTES

Palazzo Barberini

Entirely in Baroque style, this palazzo was built between 1625 and 1633, during the papacy of Urban VIII (born Maffeo Barberini), under the direction of Carlo Maderno and, later, Gian Lorenzo Bernini and Francesco Borromini. To this last artist is due the elegant helicoidal staircase, among other stunning architectural details. Awe-inspiring frescoes decorate the ceilings of the many rooms. The *Triumph of Divine Providence*, created by Pietro da Cortona between 1632 and 1639 to glorify the pope and the Barberini family, is breathtaking; also a feast for the eyes is the *Triumph of Divine Wisdom*, painted by Andrea Sacchi between 1629 and 1633. The holdings of the Galleria Nazionale d'Arte Antica (National Gallery of Ancient Art) in Palazzo Barberini include priceless artworks from the fifteenth to eighteenth centuries, including two paintings by Caravaggio (*Judith and Holofernes* and *Narcissus*), Raphael's *La Fornarina*, masterpieces by Filippo Lippi, Tintoretto, El Greco, Titian, Bronzino, and Canaletto, and paintings by the school of Giotto as well as twelfth-century works.

via delle Quattro Fontane 13
+39 06 481 45 91
open 8:30 a.m.-7 p.m. closed Mon
galleriabarberini.beniculturali.it

EATING TIP
OSTERIA
BARBERINI
via della Purificazione 21
+39 06 474 33 25
osteriabarberini.com
open 12:30-2:30 p.m.
and 6:30-10:30 p.m.
closed Sun

 4 MINUTES

Palazzo Corsini

The Corsini collection forms the main core of the Galleria Nazionale d'Arte Antica (National Gallery of Ancient Art) in Rome, Italy's first, with the only eighteenth-century Roman painting collection to have come down to us intact. Its masterpieces include works by Caravaggio, Orazio Gentileschi, Guido Reni, Guercino, and Andrea del Sarto. From 1659 onward, the palazzo was the residence of Christina, Queen of Sweden (1626–1689), who further added to the collection of precious paintings and sculptures. The queen came to Rome in 1655 after converting to Catholicism and abdicating the Swedish crown; her private apartment can still be visited today. Located in the park are Rome's Botanical Gardens, instituted in the thirteenth century and mentioned in sources that date even further back; they total nearly 30 acres and contain over 3,000 plant species, aromatic plants, aquatic plants, centuries-old trees, rose gardens, and evergreens.

via della Lungara 10; +39 06 688 02 323
open 8:30 a.m.-7:30 p.m., closed Tue
galleriacorsini.beniculturali.it
Orto Botanico largo Cristina di Svezia 24
+39 06 499 17 107
open 9 a.m.-5:30 p.m. winter;
9 a.m.-6:30 p.m summer;
web.uniroma1.it/orto botanico

In the days of Queen Christina of Sweden, the first meetings of the Accademia dell'Arcadia were held in this very garden. Among those who spent time at the palazzo (then called Riario), were Gian Lorenzo Bernini, Alessandro Scarlatti, Carlo Goldoni, and Pietro Metastasio.

EATING TIP
ENOTECA FERRARA
piazza Trilussa 41
+39 06 583 33 920
enotecaferrara.it
open 6 p.m.-2 a.m.

🚶 4 MINUTES

Palazzo Pallavicini Rospigliosi

This impressive architectural complex was built between 1605 and 1619 by Cardinal Scipione Borghese on the remains of the ancient Baths of Constantine at the Quirinal. Considered to be one of the most precious jewels of Roman Baroque style, the palazzo was acquired by Prince Rospigliosi and his consort Princess Pallavicini. The gallery, which unfortunately cannot be visited, houses about 600 paintings by such artists as Signorelli, Botticelli, Lorenzo Lotto, Rubens, and Guercino. The small museum is open to visitors, who can admire the superb collection of Renaissance and Baroque works, as well as the splendid Casino dell'Aurora, which takes its name from the ceiling fresco by Guido Reni. The Casino dell'Aurora and the garden were designed by the Flemish architect Giovanni Vasanzio. The decoration on the facade is especially beautiful, with slabs from second- and third-century Roman sarcophagi.

via XXIV Maggio 43
+39 06 481 43 44
open every first day of the month
(Closed January)
10 a.m.-12 p.m. and 3-5 p.m.
casinoaurorapallavicini.it

EATING TIP
URBANA 47
via Urbana 47
+39 06 478 84 006
urbana47.it
open 8:30 a.m.-midnight

 11 MINUTES

. PLAYLIST .

"LA DOLCE VITA"
Nino Rota

"ROMA NUN FA' LA STUPIDA STASERA"
Mina

"THAT OLD FEELING"
Chet Baker

"COME PRIMA PIÙ DI PRIMA"
Caetano Veloso

"ONE SCOTCH ONE BOURBON ONE BEER "
Amos Milburn

"UNA GIAPPONESE A ROMA"
Il Genio

"NO MORE BLUES"
Dizzy Gillespie

Welcome Home

Rome is no doubt the city with the highest number of illustrious private homes, silent witnesses to age-old and more recent memories. This tour offers the opportunity to take a trip through the different styles of everyday life, from ancient Rome to the twentieth century. It is a journey to discover the unique buildings that have marked the city's cultural life and have become famous because they were designed, commissioned, and lived in by their celebrated former inhabitants, be they emperors, artists, poets, or intellectuals. Today these sites are full-fledged museums, sagaciously combining art, architecture, design, and taste.

Casa Museo Mario Praz

Located inside the Palazzo Primoli, this house-cum-museum of the famous critic, essayist, and translator Mario Praz (1896–1982) hosts the amazing private collection of one of the most refined intellectuals to ever live in Rome. The ten rooms furnished with over 1,200 items, including paintings, sculptures, furniture, and precious objects, make up an eclectic collection of different styles, including Neoclassical and Biedermeier. The owner's intention was to fulfill the pleasure of living by being "immersed in" and not just surrounded by beauty.

Mario Praz inspired the main character of the film directed by Luchino Visconti *Conversation Piece* (1974), in which a retired professor living alone, played by Burt Lancaster, reluctantly gets dragged into the family life of the tenants living on the floor above him. The film was restored by Fendi in 2013.

via Giuseppe Zanardelli 2
+39 06 686 10 89
open Thur-Fri 2:30-7 p.m.
and Sat 9 a.m.-2 p.m.
polomusealelazio.beniculturali.it

EATING TIP
FIAMMETTA
piazza Fiammetta 10
+39 06 687 57 77
ristorantefiammetta.it
open 12:45-3 p.m. and
7-11 p.m; Wed 7-11 p.m.
closed Tue

 2 MINUTES

Domus Aurea

The Domus Aurea (Golden House), so named for the ceilings decorated in gold and precious stones and the walls clad in fine marble, is the villa built by Nero after the great fire that devastated Rome in 64 AD. To build it, the emperor expropriated a vast area of about 200 acres. The property included vineyards, meadows, and woods, and extended from the plateaus of the Palatine, Velian, Oppio, and Esquiline Hills all the way to the northwestern side of the Caelian Hill, including the lake between the highlands. Emperor Vespasian later drained the lake and built the Colosseum. Visiting what remains of the ancient Domus Aurea is a must for anyone wishing to be steeped in Rome's cultural history. Today, seeing the major restoration project under way, guided tours of the site are allowed.

via della Domus Aurea 1
+39 06 399 67 700
tours only on weekends
archeoroma.beniculturali.it

THE ADJECTIVE "GROTESQUE" COMES FROM THE WALL PAINTINGS OF THE DOMUS AUREA. DURING THE RENAISSANCE, MANY ARTISTS EXPLORED THE FRESCOED ROOMS OF THE DOMUS, BY THAT TIME UNDERGROUND, BELIEVING THEM TO BE GROTTOES. THIS EXPLAINS WHY THEY CALLED THE BIZARRE IMAGES OF FANTASTIC PLANTS, MEN, MONSTERS, AND MASKS ON THE WALLS "GROTESQUES." IN CURRENT USAGE THE WORD GROTESQUE DESCRIBES SOMETHING BIZARRE OR PECULIAR.

EATING TIP
CAFFÈ
PROPAGANDA
via Claudia 15
+39 06 945 34 255
caffepropaganda.it
open 12 p.m.-2 a.m.
closed Mon

 4 MINUTES

Domus Palazzo Valentini

The archaeological excavations under the Palazzo Valentini are now a unique permanent exhibition: via screenings, reconstructions, and simulations, visitors can experience the everyday life of an aristocratic family living in ancient Rome. This exciting multimedia experience and virtual trip through the past allows one to discover kitchens, baths, household decorations, and other furnishings via a fascinating stroll through a patrician domus (dwelling) full of mosaics, wall decorations, and polychrome floors.

via Foro Traiano 85
+ 39 06 328 10
open 9:30 a.m.-6:30 p.m., closed Tue
palazzovalentini.it

EATING TIP
LA CABANA
Via del Mancino 7/9
+39 06 679 11 90
open 12-3:30 p.m. and
7-11 p.m.
closed Sun

 5 MINUTES

Keats-Shelley House

If ever there was a place for Romantic poetry in Rome, it would undoubtedly be the Keats-Shelley House. Located at number 26 Piazza di Spagna, just opposite Pietro Bernini's Fontana della Barcaccia, this house was where John Keats lived the last years of his life, together with his friend Joseph Severn, after being advised by his physicians and friends to move to sunny Rome to treat his tuberculosis. Unfortunately, Keats's illness was already advanced, and despite treatment he died in 1821, at age 25, after months of suffering. Today the Keats-Shelley Memorial House hosts an important collection of publications on English Romanticism, as well as a museum, which preserves paintings, sculptures, mementoes, manuscripts, and first editions of the works by Keats and by the second-generation members of the movement: Percy Bysshe Shelley, Mary Shelley, and Lord Byron. Keats's grave is one of the most visited tombs in Rome's Non-Catholic Cemetery.

THE KEATS-SHELLEY HOUSE WAS SAVED FROM ABANDON THANKS TO THE AMERICAN POET ROBERT UNDERWOOD JOHNSON, WHO BROUGHT TOGETHER A GROUP OF AMERICAN, ENGLISH, AND ITALIAN INTELLECTUALS, AND IN 1906 SUCCEEDED IN COLLECTING THE FUNDS NEEDED TO ACQUIRE AND RESTORE THE HOME.

piazza di Spagna 26
+39 06 678 42 35
open10 a.m.-1 p.m. and 2-6 p.m., closed Sun
keats-shelley-house.org

EATING TIP
LA BUVETTE
via Vittoria 44
+39 06 679 03 83
open 7:30 a.m.-11 p.m.
Sun 8:30 a.m.-3 p.m.

 3 MINUTES

Museo Pietro Canonica

Situated in the park of the Villa Borghese, this museum houses a collection of works by Pietro Canonica (1869-1959), an artist distinguished for his sculpting skill and the elegance of his works. Canonica was commissioned to create monumental works, earning accolades and many prestigious acknowledgments. Upon arriving in Rome in 1922, Canonica was given use of Villa Borghese's "Fortezzuola," an abandoned park belonging to the villa, where he worked until his death. Guests can visit the seven rooms on the ground floor, the studio, and the artist's private apartment with its collection of objects, household furnishings, and paintings. Also on display are the nineteenth-century works of Piedmontese artists from the same geographical area as Canonica. The visit encompasses the private and artistic life of the sculptor, and thanks to the bronzes, marbles, maquettes, and studies on display, it gives visitors an idea of how sculpture developed during the twentieth century.

viale Pietro Canonica 2
+39 06 884 22 79
open 10 a.m.-4 p.m. winter;
1-7 p.m. summer; closed Mon
museocanonica.it

THE STUDIO IS THE SAME AS IT WAS WHEN THE ARTIST WORKED THERE. ARRANGED ON A TABLE ARE HIS WORKING TOOLS STILL COVERED IN PLASTER AND BITS OF CLAY FROM THE MAQUETTE FOR *SAN GIOVANNI BOSCO*. AT THE CENTER OF THE STUDIO IS A SCULPTOR'S EASEL ON A ROTATING BASE.

EATING TIP
MISTICANZA
via Sicilia 47
+39 06 678 61 15
misticanzaroma.it
open 7:30 a.m.- 11:30 p.m.
closed Sun

 7 MINUTES

Villino Andersen

A full-fledged studio-home, the Villino Andersen's mission is to valorize the work of the sculptor, painter, and urban designer Hendrik Christian Andersen (1872-1940), who was born in Norway and immigrated with his family to the United States, before permanently settling in Rome after a trip to Europe. At the heart of Andersen's work is the idea that monumental art is a vehicle of both harmony and peace in the world. Indeed, the artist worked on a project for an art-filled World City, which he believed would encourage humanity to pursue a state of perfection. The collection includes paintings, monumental sculptures in bronze and plaster, photographs, and other iconographic documents, bearing witness to the impressions, emotions, travels, and intense human relations that characterized this artist's life.

"I think of you all in the golden Roman air, I hang with you over your unspeakable Tiber-terrace— I sit with you in those noble chambers," wrote Henry James to his friend Hendrik in 1912.

via Pasquale Stanislao Mancini 20
+39 06 321 90 89
open 9 a.m.-7:30 p.m., closed Mon
polomusealelazio.beniculturali.it

Eating Tip
Settembrini Caffé
via Luigi Settembrini 19/27
+39 06 976 10 325
viasettembrini.com
open 7 a.m.-1:30 a.m.
Sun 8 a.m.-1:30 a.m.

 8 MINUTES

. PLAYLIST .

"TIME"
Monodeluxe
(Aqua Bassino Remix)

"UNTER"
Nils Frahm

" HANKY PANKY "
St Germain

"QUE SERA"
Wax Taylor

" CARBONATED"
Mount Kimbie

"DON'T WORRY"
Andrea Rango
(Horatio Badass remix)

"THIRTEEN THIRTYFIVE"
Dillon

A Thrill
of a Tour

———————●———————

A tour whose aim is to discover parts of Rome that are unusual, often underground, at times mysterious, and even esoteric or macabre. Seven intriguing sites where spirituality, art, cult, and magic are often intertwined. Places whose symbolism may be pagan or Christian, or related to ancient and distant cultures. Places where one discovers peace while walking undisturbed, or, like in a treasure hunt, the traces of a social history that was more complex than might be imagined. These are places that tell us that Rome does not have just one soul, but many all at the same time, and all of which deserve to be explored.

CAMPO VERANO

Always a burial site, the ancient field that runs along the Via Consolare Tiburtina and that at one time belonged to the Verani, an important family in the Roman Senate in the age of the Roman Republic, was instituted as a cemetery in the early nineteenth century during Napoleon's reign, when it was established that burials had to take place outside the city walls. Designed by Giuseppe Valadier, featuring an imposing entrance decorated with large statues representing Meditation, Hope, Charity, and Silence, the cemetery is known for its long and silent pathways and its sepulchral art, which makes Campo Verano an open-air museum. Under the auspices of the City of Rome, themed visits free of charge guide visitors in their discovery of illustrious names on the graves—made by equally famous master sculptors—of inestimable historical, artistic, and cultural value.

piazzale del Verano 1
+39 06 492 36 331
open Mon-Fri 8:30 a.m.-2 p.m.,
closed Sat and Sun
cimitericapitolini.it

EATING TIP
SAID
via Tiburtina 135
+39 06 446 92 04
said.it
Mon 7:30 p.m.-12:30 a.m.
Tue Wed Thurs
10 a.m.-12:30 a.m.
Fri Sat 10 a.m.-1:30 a.m.
Sun 10 a.m.-midnight
🚶 3 MINUTES

THE CATACOMBS OF SAINT SEBASTIAN

The Latin word *catacumba* comes from the Greek *katá kymbés*, literally "near the hollows," and it indicates a sunken area formed by the ancient mines of tuff along the Via Appia Antica (Appian Way). The quarry, used by Christians mainly to bury slaves and freedmen, was called *cemetery*, meaning "place of rest." Also preserved here for a time were the relics of the apostles Peter and Paul; after the deposition of the body of the martyred Sebastian, the catacombs underwent a period of great development, which involved the construction of numerous galleries. The great variety of decorations is worth noting: each tomb bears a sign so that it can be recognized.

THE STONES CHOSEN FOR A CATACOMB WERE BASED ON A FAMILY'S WEALTH: THEY WERE RARELY MADE OF MARBLE, MORE FREQUENTLY OF TERRACOTTA, AND THE CONSUL'S NAME WAS STAMPED ON THEM. IT WAS THESE STAMPS THAT LATER ALLOWED THE STONES TO BE DATED.

EATING TIP
RISTORANTE
L'ARCHEOLOGIA
via Appia Antica 139
+39 06 788 04 94
larcheologia.com
open 12:30-3 p.m.
and 8-11 p.m.

 2 MINUTES

via Appia Antica 136
+39 06 785 03 50
open 10 a.m.-4:30 p.m., closed Sun
catacombe.org

THE MAGIC PORTAL OF PIAZZA VITTORIO

The Alchemical Door, also known as the Magic Portal, was located at the entrance to the esoteric laboratory of Massimiliano Palombara (1614–1680), marquess of Pietraforte. Palombara was famous for his passion for the esoteric sciences and the occult practices that took place in his villa in the countryside east of Rome, on the Esquiline Hill. Legend has it that one of Palombara's friends managed to turn lead into gold, but before sharing the secret he disappeared through the Alchemical Door. However, he did leave a mysterious paper filled with riddles and symbols that allegedly contained the secret of the philosopher's stone. Unable to decipher them, and hoping that sooner or later he would succeed in doing so, the marquess had them carved on the portal.

INSCRIBED AT THE THRESHOLD ARE THE WORDS *SI SEDES NON IS*, A PALINDROME THAT CAN BE READ FORWARD AS "IF YOU SIT, DO NOT GO" AND BACKWARD AS "IF YOU DO NOT SIT, GO."

giardini di piazza Vittorio Emanuele II
prolocoroma.it

EATING TIP
LA BOTTEGA
DEL CAFFÈ
piazza della Madonna
dei Monti 5
+39 06 474 15 78
open 8 a.m.-2 a.m.

 8 MINUTES

THE MITHRAEUM OF SANTA PRISCA

With its expansion to Persian lands, Rome witnessed the spread of the cult of the Indo-Iranian pagan god Mithras, venerated to such a degree by some emperors that Mithraism became an official religion. The god of light, protector of peace, justice, and treaties, Mithras was worshipped by soldiers, too. By analogy with the grotto where Christ was born, worship in the Hellenistic-Roman world took place in the *mithraeum*: this was a windowless room often made out of underground spaces such as baths, hypogea, or the areas below private homes. It no doubt was a good hiding place for followers of Mithraism when Christianity became the empire's official religion. The Mithraeum of Santa Prisca, created out of a private home in the first century AD, was discovered in 1934. The church that stands over it (Santa Prisca) was most likely built by Christians who sought to eliminate all trace of the earlier pagan worship.

via Santa Prisca 8
+39 06 574 37 98
reservations only or
2nd and 4th Saturdays of each month
archeoroma.beniculturali.it

THE MITHRAEUM USUALLY FEATURES AN ENTRANCE THAT IS SEPARATED FROM THE VESTIBULE, A RECTANGULAR CAVERN KNOWN AS THE *SPELAEUM* OR *SPELUNCA*, WITH SEATING TO THE SIDES FOR THE RITUAL BANQUET CALLED THE *AGAPE*; IT ALSO HAS A SANCTUARY LOCATED IN A NICHE BEHIND THE ALTAR. PAINTED ON THE CEILING IS A STARRY SKY WITH THE ZODIAC AND PLANETS.

EATING TIP
THE CORNER RESTAURANT
viale Aventino 121
+39 06 455 97 350
thecornerrome.com/restaurant
open 12:30-3 p.m. and
7:30-11 p.m. closed Sun

 4 MINUTES

THE NON-CATHOLIC CEMETERY

Behind the Pyramid of Cestius, on the western side of the Testaccio quarter, is the Non-Catholic Cemetery, also known as the English Cemetery. In addition to the significant number of Protestant and Eastern Orthodox graves, there are also graves pertaining to Islamism, Zoroastrianism, Buddhism, and Confucianism. The Protestant religion requires that the deceased be buried in the ground, surrounded by pine trees, cypresses, myrtle and laurel trees, wild roses and camellias. Strolling around the grounds of the Non-Catholic Cemetery one may "encounter" gravestones bearing names of international fame, among them Julius Goethe, son of the poet; the German writer Malwida von Meysenbug; the Romantic poets John Keats, Percy Bysshe Shelley, and John Severn; the founder of the Italian Communist Party Antonio Gramsci; the Beat Generation poet Gregory Corso; and Irene Galitzine, a 1960s fashion designer famous for inventing "palazzo pyjamas."

via Caio Cestio 6
+ 39 06 574 19 00
open 9 a.m.-5 p.m.,
Sun and holidays 9 a.m.-1 p.m.
cemeteryrome.it

EATING TIP
FELICE
via Mastro Giorgio 29
+39 06 574 68 00
feliceatestaccio.it
open 12:30-3 p.m.
and 7:30-11:15 p.m.

 5 MINUTES

THE PYRAMID OF CESTIUS

The Pyramid of Cestius is the only funerary monument to have survived among the many such pyramid-shaped structures built in the first century BC, after the conquest of Egypt. Caius (Gaius) Cestius, a wealthy senior Roman magistrate, ordered in his will that his tomb be erected in the shape of a pyramid within 330 days of his death, otherwise his heirs would lose all rights to his estate. The tomb was quickly built along the Via Ostiense and later set into the Aurelian Wall. Measuring a total of 120 feet in height and with a base of 99 feet per side, it is clad in white (Lunense) marble. According to Egyptian tradition, the large burial chamber was walled at the time of burial; the first looting of the tomb took place in the Middle Ages, when the cinerary urn and most of the decorations were stolen.

THE USE OF CONCRETE ALLOWED THE ROMANS TO BUILD A PYRAMID WITH A MORE ACUTE ANGLE THAN THE TRADITIONAL EGYPTIAN PYRAMID, RESULTING IN A SLEEKER AND PROPORTIONATELY TALLER STRUCTURE.

via Raffaele Persichetti
+39 06 399 67 700
reservations only Sat and Sun
archeoroma.beniculturali.it

EATING TIP
RISTORANTE
CONSOLINI
via Marmorata 28
+39 06 573 00 148
ristoranteconsolini.it
open 12 a.m.-3 p.m.
and 7:30 p.m.-midnight
closed Mon

 9 MINUTES

SANTA MARIA DELLA CONCEZIONE

The church of Santa Maria della Concezione, on Via Veneto, was built close to the family palazzo by Pope Urban VIII Barberini for his brother Antonio, a member of the religious order of the Capuchins. Formed by a small nave with five chapels on either side, the church houses relics, illustrious tombs, and important masterpieces, including paintings by Pietro da Cortona and Domenichino. Of particular interest is the crypt beneath the church. All the wall decorations and even the lamps, in Rococo style, are made from bones removed from the mass grave in the old cemetery. In fact, the bones of at least 4,000 Capuchin monks, along with those of many other monks and poor Romans who died between 1528 and 1870.

BE SURE TO LOOK AT GUIDO RENI'S 1635 PAINTING *THE ARCHANGEL MICHAEL* TO GLIMPSE A POPE WITH SATAN'S FACE! THE ANGEL CRUSHES LUCIFER, WHOSE FACE IS THAT OF GIOVANNI BATTISTA PAMPHILJ, WHO IN 1644 WOULD BE ELECTED INNOCENT X.

via Vittorio Veneto 27
+39 06 888 03 695
open 9 a.m.-7 p.m.
cappucciniviaveneto.it

EATING TIP
MOMA
via san Basilio 42
+39 06 420 11 798
ristorantemoma.it
open 12:30-3 p.m.
and 7:30 p.m.-midnight
closed Sun

 4 MINUTES

WONDER
IS THE PURPOSE
OF ART

Shrinking what is large and enlarging what is small, moving an image away or bringing it in close, making people believe what doesn't exist, and transforming reality through optical illusion and tricking the senses. Art has always used such techniques to fool both the eye and the mind. Let yourselves be tempted by the clever use of lines, proportions, and colors; you will inevitably fall into the trap of the oddities and virtuosities of art and architecture. Such is the key to this intriguing tour, which allows visitors to become familiar with seven Roman masterpieces from different eras. Trompe l'œil paintings dating from antiquity to the present tantalize the eyes, heightening and kindling the desire for discovery.

. PLAYLIST .

"Í DANSI MEð ÞÉR"
Björk

"PARADISCO"
Charlotte Gainsbourg

"A REAL HERO"
College (feat. Electric Youth)

"1980"
Flavia Lazzarini

"MUMBAY DISCO SENSATION"
Unouzbeck & Venturi

"HIGH AS THE SUN"
Haty Haty

"THE WINTER HYMN"
Pantha du Prince (feat. Queens)

ARMANDO TROVAJOLI MUSIC BRIDGE

The Music Bridge is a perfect example of contemporary architecture in the city. Made of steel and reinforced concrete, this curved and arched suspension bridge over the Tiber River connects the Della Vittoria and Flaminio quarters and is reserved for cyclists, pedestrians, and public transportation. A project by the London studio Buro Happold and the engineer Davood Liaghat, along with Kit Powell-Williams Architects, it was inaugurated in 2011. Since 2013 it has been named for Armando Trovajoli, one of the major pianists, composers, and orchestra directors who was born and lived in Rome. Trovajoli was also the composer of many soundtracks for films directed by such filmmakers as Vittorio De Sica, Dino Risi, and Ettore Scola.

EATING TIP
BAR DUE FONTANE
piazza Perin del Vaga 13
+39 06 324 07 86
open 7 a.m.-7 p.m.
closed Sun

lungotevere Flaminio
at piazza Gentile da Fabriano

🏃 4 MINUTES

Auditorium Parco della Musica

Opened in 2002, this multifunctional complex dedicated to music was designed by the architect Renzo Piano. It hosts the city's most prestigious events, and its rich calendar includes sacred music, chamber music, and contemporary music. Three huge rooms resembling sound boxes are located in the large park of the Flaminio quarter, surrounded by luxuriant vegetation that echoes the emotions evoked by the music. The materials are those of Roman tradition: travertine for the seating section, the foyer, and the entrances; Roman brick for the vertical surfaces; cherry wood for the interiors, guaranteeing high-quality acoustics. Technology and design have contributed to the great success of this temple of music. It is the number-one cultural venue in Europe in terms of visitors, and second in the world after Lincoln Center in New York.

THOUGH THEIR SHAPES RECALL THE ARMOR OF AN ARMADILLO OR A SCARAB (WHICH IS HOW THEY ARE REFERRED TO), THE AUDITORIUM'S THREE HUGE SHELLS WERE INSPIRED BY THE SOUND BOX OF THE LUTE.

viale Pietro de Coubertin 28
+39 06 802 41 281
open winter 11 a.m.-6 p.m.,
Sun and holidays 10 a.m.-6 p.m;
summer 11 a.m.-8 p.m.,
Sun and holidays 10 a.m.-8 p.m.
auditorium.com

EATING TIP
RED RESTAURANT & DESIGN
viale Pietro de Coubertin 12/16
+39 06 806 91 630
redrestaurant.roma.it
open 9 a.m.-2 a.m.

🏃 2 MINUTES

Basilica of San Clemente

A visit to the Basilica of San Clemente, famous for its marvelous mosaics and its chapel decorated with fifteenth-century frescoes, is truly a journey through time. The surprising layers of buildings allow visitors to discover about 1,300 years of Roman civil and religious history, from the Republican age to medieval times. The Basilica Superiore, which is visible from the street, is dedicated to Clement, the fourth pope (r. 88–97), and was built in the twelfth century over the remains of the Basilica Inferiore, dated to about 350; below that are other buildings, including a third-century mithraeum. And discovered even deeper down are the remains of a building that was at one time a Roman patrician home, as well as a group of Roman buildings from the post-Neronian period.

The Basilica Inferiore contains one of the first written examples of vernacular Italian. Under the fresco that tells the legend of Sisinno, a Roman prefect, is a "comic strip" with phrases in the vernacular, commonly spoken at the time but never used in written texts.

via Labicana 95
+39 06 774 00 21
open 9 a.m.-12:30 p.m. and 3-6 p.m.,
Sun and holidays 12:15-6 p.m.
basilicasanclemente.com

Eating Tip
Tempio di Iside, Cottura 0°
via Labicana 50
angolo via Pietro Verri
+39 06 700 47 41
isideristorante.it
open 12:30-3 p.m. and
7-11:30 p.m. closed Sun

 4 MINUTES

CHURCH OF SANT'IGNAZIO IN CAMPO MARZIO

Dedicated to Saint Ignatius of Loyola, founder of the Society of Jesus, this church is one of the finest, most virtuosic examples of Roman Baroque style, especially in its use of perspective. Andrea Pozzo's decoration from late 1600 seems to break through the ceiling; this colossal illusionistic image was meant to exalt the religious society's apostolic activity. Double-height columns and arches also characterize this church, as do the painted architectural elements. The way the ceiling opens up into an infinite space was originally meant to suggest the continuity between Earth and Heaven, between the human world and divine reality. Vistors can stand at a specific location on the floor to observe a painting on canvas reproducing the artificial dome at the intersection of the transept.

AND THERE ARE OTHER ILLUSIONS TO BEDAZZLE YOU HERE AS WELL: FIND THE TWO MARBLE DISCS ON THE FLOOR OF THE CENTRAL NAVE AND STAND RIGHT THERE. NOW LOOK UP!

via del Caravita 8/a
+39 06 679 44 06
open 7:30 a.m.-7 p.m.,
Sun and holidays 9 a.m.-7 p.m.
santignazio.gesuiti.it

EATING TIP
GINGER
via Borgognona 43/44
+39 06 699 40 836
www.ginger.roma.it
open 10 a.m.-1 a.m.

 9 MINUTES

COPPEDÈ QUARTER

Situated in the Trieste quarter, between Piazza Buenos Aires and Via Tagliamento, is a group of buildings—over forty, including palazzi and *villini*—arranged around Piazza Mincio. At the center is the Fontana delle Rane, an imposing fountain decorated with twelve frogs; it is the one the Beatles "took a dip in" after their performance at the nearby Piper Club. Built in the early decades of the twentieth century, the neighborhood takes its name from the eclectic architect who designed it, Gino Coppedè. It is a mixture of architectural oddities blending Italian Liberty style and Art Déco with Greek, medieval, Baroque, Assyrian-Babylonian art, and even cinema (such as the arch that reproduces a scene from the 1914 film *Cabiria*, at number 2 Piazza Mincio). Owing to its unique architecture, the Coppedè quarter has often been chosen as a set by filmmakers: among them, Dario Argento for *Inferno* and *The Bird with the Crystal Plumage* (*L'uccello dalle piume di cristallo*), and Richard Donner for *The Omen*.

THIS ROMAN DISTRICT IS SO MAGICAL, ONE RISKS LOSING ALL NOTION OF TIME. TO MAKE SURE THAT DOESN'T HAPPEN TO YOU, KEEP AN EYE ON THE MAGNIFICENT FRESCOES, INCLUDING A MERIDIAN, ON THE BACK OF THE CASA DELLE FATE.

EATING TIP
DIETRO LE QUINTE
via Tirso 85
+39 06 454 21 672
dietrolequinteroma.it
Mon-Fri 6:30 a.m.-midnight
Sat 7 a.m.-midnight
closed Sun

 4 MINUTES

piazza Mincio

PALAZZETTO DELLO SPORT

The conception for this indoor arena dates to the mid-1950s and was part of the overall plan for the 1960 Rome Olympics. It was commissioned from the architect Annibale Vitellozzi, who in turn was assisted by the engineer Pier Luigi Nervi in the creation of the thin-shell reinforced concrete dome. Completed in just thirty days, the futuristic dome, with its ribbed pattern of triangular and rhomboidal elements, was made of ferrocement, a system that Nervi had patented in 1943. Owing to its perfect symmetry and modern virtuosity, the Palazzetto dello Sport is still considered an unparalleled example of architecture. "A huge Medusa" and a "squashed Pantheon" are two examples of the imagery used by the architect Bruno Zevi to describe the figurative, plastic, and dynamic force of Nervi and Vitellozzi's building, in which the natural lighting that filters between the intertwining structural weavings multiplies the interior space in an illusionistic manner.

EATING TIP
LOLA
via Flaminia 305
+39 06 321 92 79
lolaroma.it
Tue-Sun 7 a.m.-2 a.m.
Mon 7 a.m.-4 p.m.

🚶 6 MINUTES

piazza Apollodoro 10

Palazzo Spada and the Colonnaded Gallery

A veritable jewel hidden in the secret garden of Palazzo Spada, the Colonnaded Gallery was commissioned in the mid-seventeenth century by Cardinal Bernardino Spada from the architect Francesco Borromini, who was assisted by a mathematician, Father Giovanni Maria da Bitonto. What's particular about the structure is its illusory depth: although it appears to be 100 feet long, in actual fact it doesn't exceed 30 feet. The artificial perspective is the result of the convergence of planes into a single vanishing point: the ceiling, which comes downward, and the mosaic floor, which moves upward, accentuate the illusion of a long covered path toward the garden. The gallery, in turn, houses a sculpture that appears to be life-size, but is really no more than 24 inches tall. After the illusion, go back to reality by immersing yourself in the very colorful market of the Campo de' Fiori, whose fragrances welcome visitors every morning (except Sundays).

On the first floor of the palazzo is a colossal sculpture of Pompey. They say it is the one at whose feet Julius Caesar fell, stabbed twenty-three times by his conspirators.

piazza Capodiferro 13,
vicolo del Polverone 15B
+39 06 687 48 96
open 8:30 a.m.-7:30 p.m., closed Tue
galleriaborghese.it/galleriaSpada.html

Eating Tip
Dar Filettaro
largo dei Librari 88
+39 06 686 40 18
open 5-11:40 p.m.
closed Sun

 3 MINUTES

. PLAYLIST .

"FAMILY PORTRAIT"
Rachel's

"FORBIDDEN COLOURS"
Ryuichi Sakamoto

"THE AURAL TRICK"
Wim Mertens

"LAND OF ALL"
Woodkid

"ARABESQUE N. 1 - ANDANTINO CON MOTO"
Claude Debussy

"STRINGS OF LIFE"
Francesco Tristano

"FOUR"
Ólafur Arnalds & Nils Frahm

CARAVAGGIO
IN ROME

Our search for Caravaggio in Rome takes us back to the period between the sixteenth and seventeenth centuries and the capital's most characteristic sites, to the years when the star of Michelangelo Merisi, aka Caravaggio, shone a dramatic and theatrical light. A restless, turbulent soul, forever pursued by the law owing to the many arguments and fights he got into—he was even accused of murder—it was in Rome that Caravaggio received the first plaudits for his talent as a painter, one who was to have a huge impact on the Baroque period. Caravaggio's fame grew in the parlors of the Roman aristocracy, and at least twenty of the masterpieces he was commissioned to make in Rome are still here to see.

THE CYCLE OF SAINT MATTHEW

These three masterpieces—*Saint Matthew and the Angel*, *The Martyrdom of Saint Matthew*, and *The Vocation of Saint Matthew*—are preserved in the church of San Luigi dei Francesi (Saint Louis of the French), in the chapel that Cardinal Mathieu Cointrel (known as Contarelli in Italy) acquired in 1565. This pictorial cycle was Caravaggio's first important Roman cycle, and it marked a turning point in his exploration of the use of light. Seen here is the birth of his legendary chiaroscuro technique, and indeed the scene is illuminated in situ by a beam of light from a source outside the picture plane, leaving part of the painting in a mysterious half-light of great realism.

IF THE VISIT HAS WORKED UP YOUR APPETITE, OVERLOOKING THE PIAZZA IS THE PALAZZO WHERE MARCHIONESS ELISABETTA PATRIZI MONTORO ORGANIZES ONE- OR TWO-DAY COOKING COURSES FOR A MAXIMUM OF TEN PARTICIPANTS. RESERVATIONS ARE REQUIRED WELL IN ADVANCE.
(+39 06 879 01 173 , +39 347 547 65 34, PALAZZOPATRIZI.IT).

San Luigi dei Francesi
piazza San Luigi dei Francesi
+39 06 688 271
open 9:30 a.m.-1 p.m.
Sat 9:30 a.m.-12:30 p.m.
Sun 11:30 a.m.-1 p.m.
saintlouis-rome.net

EATING TIP
LA ROSETTA
via della Rosetta 8/9
+39 06 686 10 02
larosettaristorante.it
open
12 a.m.-11 p.m.

🚶 2 MINUTES

THE ENTOMBMENT

The Entombment of Christ (1600–1604), one of the works that Napoleon had transferred to France in 1797, and was returned to Italy in 1816, is now on view in the Vatican Museums. Considered to be one of Caravaggio's finest works, it was commissioned by Girolamo Vittrice to be placed on the altar of the family chapel in the church of Santa Maria in Vallicella. Akin to Michelangelo's *Pietà* in Saint Peter's, Caravaggio created a scene that departed from the traditional iconography of the time. The artist chose instead to represent the moment when Nicodemus and John laid the body on the bare stone, where it was anointed by fragrant oil before being buried.

THIS PAINTING EXUDES A PROFOUND SENSE OF SPIRITUALITY, VISIBLE IN THE FACE OF NICODEMUS AND EVEN MORE SO IN THE DIGNIFIED EXPRESSION OF PAIN FELT BY BOTH THE VIRGIN AND MARY MAGDALENE. THE COUNTER-REFORMATION REQUIRED THAT SACRED ART FEATURE IMAGES THAT WERE CLEAR, AND THAT THEY EXPRESS THE MOST SPIRITUAL MEANING OF THE HOLY SCRIPTURES.

EATING TIP
LA ZANZARA
via Crescenzio 84
+39 06 683 92 227
lazanzararoma.com
open 8 a.m.-2 a.m.

 8 MINUTES

Musei Vaticani
viale Vaticano
+39 06 698 84 676
open 9 a.m.-6 p.m.,
and the last Sun of the month
museivaticani.va

THE FORTUNE TELLER, SAINT JOHN THE BAPTIST

Two of Caravaggio's paintings are housed at the Pinacoteca (Painting Gallery) of the Capitoline Museums. *The Fortune Teller*, made between 1593 and 1594, is a genre painting (a cunning gypsy, while telling an ingenuous knight his fortune, manages to steal the ring from his finger) describing the everyday life of the alleyways in the heart of Rome. Another version of this work can be seen in the Louvre Museum in Paris. The second canvas by Caravaggio on display here is *Saint John the Baptist*, or *Youth with Ram*, of 1602, one of two copies of this work (the other is at the Galleria Doria Pamphilj). It was commissioned by the Mattei family for their private residence, and its composition reminds us of the naked figures painted by Michelangelo on the ceiling of the Sistine Chapel.

LEGEND HAS IT THAT TO PAINT THE *FORTUNE TELLER* CARAVAGGIO CHOSE A WOMAN PASSING BY HIS STUDIO WHO REALLY WAS A GYPSY AS A MODEL.

Musei Capitolini
piazza del Campidoglio 1
+39 06 06 08
open 9:30 a.m.-7:30 p.m.
museicapitolini.org

EATING TIP
LA TAVERNA
DEL GHETTO
via del Portico d'Ottavia 8
+39 06 688 09 771
latavernadelghetto.com
Sun-Thur 12 a.m.-11 p.m.
Fri 12-3 p.m. Sat 6-11 p.m.

 10 MINUTES

JUPITER, NEPTUNE, PLUTO

The casino of Villa Ludovisi, near Porta Pinciana, houses the painting *Jupiter, Neptune, Pluto* (1597), Caravaggio's only mural painting. It was commissioned by his Roman patron, Cardinal Francesco Maria del Monte, who dabbled in alchemy and thus believed that all natural things are derived from a triad of elements: Jupiter/Air, Pluto/Earth, Neptune/Water, the personifications of sulfur, chloride, and mercury, and the three states of matter (gas, solid, and liquid). Caravaggio arranged them around a celestial sphere studded with the signs of the zodiac, portraying them from the unusual perspective of an observer who gazes at them from below. Legend has it that to represent this complex scene, the artist used a large flat mirror on which he posed naked.

DON'T MISS THE CHANCE TO TAKE A WALK ALONG THE AVENUES OF THE PINCIAN HILL TO LOOK FOR THE 224 BUSTS OF FAMOUS PEOPLE, INCLUDING ARTISTS, LITERATI, SCIENTISTS, AND MORE. ARE YOU FAMILIAR WITH THEM ALL?

Casino Boncompagni Ludovisi
Villa Ludovisi
via Lombardia 46
+39 06 483 942
reservations required
Mon-Wed-Fri 9 a.m.-1:30 p.m.
prolocoroma.it/casino-dell-aurora-roma-villaludovisi

EATING TIP
L.A.VI. VINERIA LATTERIA
via Tomacelli 23
+39 06 454 27 760
la-vi.it
open 8:30 a.m.-2 a.m.

🚕 9 MINUTES

MADONNA AND CHILD WITH SAINT ANNE

The *Madonna dei Palafrenieri*, or *Madonna and Child with Saint Anne* (1605–06), was found to be unacceptable and therefore rejected by the Brotherhood of the Palafrenieri in Saint Peter's. The reasons they gave were the Virgin's low neckline, the Christ Child's age (he was too old to be portrayed naked), and his excessive involvement in the portrayal of the killing of the serpent. Not to mention the problem of Caravaggio's chosen model, a well-known Roman prostitute. The work was acquired by Cardinal Borghese and is preserved in the Galleria Borghese, along with other masterpieces by Caravaggio: *Boy with a Basket of Fruit* (1593–94), *Young Sick Bacchus* (ca. 1593), *Saint Jerome* (ca. 1606), *Saint John the Baptist* (ca. 1610), and *David with the Head of Goliath* (1609–10).

EATING TIP
IL COVO
RISTOBISTROT
via Brescia 20
+39 06 902 38 528
open 11 a.m.-11 p.m.
closed Sun

🚶 10 MINUTES

Galleria Borghese
piazzale Scipione Borghese 5
+39 06 841 65 42
open 9 a.m.-7 p.m., closed Mon
galleriaborghese.beniculturali.it

Madonna of the Pilgrims

The famous *Madonna of the Pilgrims* (or of Loreto; 1604–06) hangs above the altar of the Cavalletti Chapel, the first chapel on the left in the church of Sant'Agostino in Campo Marzio. The work was commissioned by Ermete Cavalletti, an officer of the Papal States. The Virgin's physical features, inspired by Classical models, clash with the crude realism of the pilgrims: the poverty of the two figures in the foreground is emphasized by the man's muddy feet and the woman's shabby, soiled bonnet. The allusion is to the lack of balance between the wealth of the Church and the suffering of humanity, to whom the Virgin reveals herself.

To get an idea of the Colosseum's original appearance take a look at the facade of the church of Sant'Agostino in Campo Marzio. The travertine slabs that now clad it once covered the Roman amphitheatre, which was later used as a "quarry" from which to take materials to build the church.

EATING TIP
CAFFÈ NOVECENTO
via del Governo Vecchio 12
+39 06 686 52 42
open 9 a.m.-10 p.m.

 7 MINUTES

Sant'Agostino in Campo Marzio
piazza Sant'Agostino
+39 06 688 01 962
open 7:45 a.m.-12 p.m. and 4-8 p.m.
vicariatusurbis.org

Narcissus at the Fountain

The Galleria Nazionale d'Arte Antica (National Gallery of Ancient Art) houses *Judith Beheading Holofernes* (1597–1600), *Saint Francis in Meditation* (1606), and *Narcissus at the Fountain* (1597–99); the attribution of this last painting, perhaps Caravaggio's most hermetic work, was at the heart of heated debate. However, restoration carried out in 1995 confirmed that the painting was made by Caravaggio, probably during a phase when he was changing his style. Caravaggio chose to tell the myth of Narcissus in his own way, based on Ovid's *Metamorphoses*: a young man who was in love with his appearance stopped to look at his reflection in a pool, and while trying to grasp the image he fell in and was transformed into the eponymous flower.

AT ONE TIME THE GARDEN OF PALAZZO BARBERINI WAS A PARK THAT STRETCHED FROM VIA XX SETTEMBRE TO VIA DI SAN NICOLA DA TOLENTINO. BESIDES THE ITALIAN-STYLE GARDEN AND THE SECRET GARDEN THERE WAS ALSO A GARDEN OF EXOTIC ANIMALS, INCLUDING OSTRICHES AND CAMELS.

Palazzo Barberini
via delle Quattro Fontane 13
+39 06 481 45 91
open 8:30 a.m. -7 p.m. closed Mon
galleriabarberini.beniculturali.it

EATING TIP
PANELLA
via Merulana 54
+39 06 487 24 35
panellaroma.com
Mon Tue Wed Thur
8 a.m.-11 p.m.
Fri Sat 8 a.m.-midnight
Sun 8 a.m.-4 p.m.

 6 MINUTES

REST ON THE FLIGHT INTO EGYPT

Exhibited in the Galleria Doria Pamphilj are the *Penitent Magdalene* (1594–95), the *Rest on the Flight into Egypt* (1595–96), and one of the two almost identical copies of *Saint John the Baptist* or *Youth with Ram* (both made in 1602; the other is in the Capitoline Museums). The *Rest on the Flight into Egypt* is one of young Caravaggio's masterpieces. The artist arranged the composition so that the angel is seen from behind; he also distributed the light in a unique way, careful to avoid the dramatic tones achieved with the chiaroscuro effect in many of his other works. Nature and landscape play an important role: to the left are dry branches, while luxuriant greenery surrounds the Virgin and Child, including symbolic plants such as laurel, thistle, and common mullein. According to the critic Maurizio Calvesi, the painting alludes to the salvation of Christians, who may achieve beatitude thanks to their faith.

IN THE GALLERIA DORIA PAMPHILJ DON'T MISS THE OUTSTANDING *PORTRAIT OF INNOCENT X* BY DIEGO VELÁZQUEZ, WHICH THE POPE HIMSELF, IN THE WORLD, GIOVANNI BATTISTA PAMPHILJ, SAID WAS "TOO TRUE TO LIFE." THE SITTER'S "SATIRICAL, SATURNAL, COARSE, AND VERY UGLY" APPEARANCE IS REMARKABLY SIMILAR TO THE FACE OF SATAN PORTRAYED BY GUIDO RENI IN SANTA MARIA DELLA CONCEZIONE.

EATING TIP
SALOTTO 42
piazza di Pietra 42
+39 06 678 58 04
salotto42.space.it
open 10 a.m.-2 a.m.

 4 MINUTES

Galleria Doria Pamphilj
via del Corso 305
+39 06 679 73 23
open 9 a.m.-7 p.m.
doriapamphilj.it

SAINT JOHN THE BAPTIST

This painting is undoubtedly one of the lesser known versions of this subject according to Caravaggio. The painting joined the Corsini collection in 1784 as *S. Giovanni Battista. Stile di Caravaggio* (Saint John the Baptist. In the Style of Caravaggio) and it is for this reason that for a long time there were doubts concerning the work's authenticity. Today the attribution has also been confirmed by X-radiography as well as by the many similarities in composition when compared with the *Saint John the Baptist*, also by Caravaggio, housed at the Nelson-Atkins Museum of Art, Kansas City. In addition to the characteristic style of light, barely visible in the background is a tree trunk, an element that was often present in the artist's works from his final Roman period. The work is on view on the first floor of Palazzo Corsini, the location, along with Palazzo Barberini, of the Galleria Nazionale d'Arte Antica.

PALAZZO CORSINI WAS COMMISSIONED BY THE FLORENTINE FAMILY TO CELEBRATE CARDINAL LORENZO'S ELECTION TO POPE IN 1730, UNDER THE NAME OF CLEMENT XII.

Palazzo Corsini - Galleria Nazionale di Arte Antica
Via della Lungara 10
+39 06 688 02 323
open 8:30 a.m.-7:30 p.m. closed Tue
galleriacorsini.beniculturali.it

EATING TIP
CANTINA RIPAGRANDE
via di San Francesco
a Ripa 73
+39 06 454 76 237
open
12:30 p.m.-2 a.m.
closed Sun

🚶 12 MINUTES

SAINT PAUL AND SAINT PETER

The Basilica of Santa Maria del Popolo is one of the finest examples of the Roman Renaissance. In addition to later contributions by Bramante, Raphael, and Bernini, it hosts in one of its most important chapels, the Cerasi Chapel, two canvases painted by Caravaggio between 1600 and 1601: *Conversion of Saint Paul* and *Crucifixion of Saint Peter*. Both works, in addition to revealing Caravaggio's immense talent as a painter, also show his outstanding skill at conferring historical accuracy to sacred themes, achieved through the strong chromatic contrast, extreme realism of the details, and physicality of the subjects. Above the chapel altar is the *Assumption of the Virgin* by Annibale Carracci, another masterpiece from the same period.

IN THE GOLDEN BAS-RELIEF BENEATH THE ALTAR CEILING, LOOK FOR THE WITCHES DANCING AROUND A WALNUT TREE, THE POPE HOLDING A HOE, AND A SKELETON IN A HOLE. THESE IMAGES ILLUSTRATE THE LEGEND OF POPE PASCHAL II, WHO PURIFIED THE AREA BY DIGGING UP NERO'S SKELETON BURIED UNDER THE WALNUT TREE THAT WAS LOCATED EXACTLY WHERE THE CHURCH NOW STANDS.

Santa Maria del Popolo
piazza del Popolo 12
+39 06 361 08 36
Mon-Thur 10:30 a.m.-12:30 p.m. and
4-6:30 p.m., Fri-Sat 10:30 a.m.-6:30 p.m.,
Sun 4:30-6:30 p.m.
vicariatusurbis.org

EATING TIP
BAR ROSATI
piazza del Popolo 5
+39 06 322 58 59
barrosati.com
open 7:30 a.m.-11 p.m.

 2 MINUTES

. Playlist .

"RUNNING UP THAT HILL"
Chromatics

"UNA SETTIMANA"
Flavia Lazzarini

"CAN'T HELP IT"
Michael Jackson (Tangoterje remix)

"TUTTO BENE"
Jolly Mare

"LOUD PLACES"
Jamie xx (feat. Romy)

"SUNNY"
Pillowtalk

"CAN'T DO WITHOUT YOU"
Caribou

From Modernity to Metaphysics

Rome and metaphysics: these two words merge the origins of the city and the "new" Rome of the early twentieth century. Before us is the Rationalist architecture of the EUR district and of the Foro Italico, which were meant to convey a sense of grandeur, order, and solidity, visible in their symmetry and in the evident nod to Classical sculpture. But even before these buildings were made, this same theme was expressed in the works of Giorgio de Chirico, the pre-eminent master of Metaphysics. Visitors will experience the novelties and the symbolic allusions to imperial glory in the thinking and imagination of the first half of the twentieth century.

Casa Fondazione Giorgio de Chirico

It was on the top three floors of the Palazzetto dei Borgognoni that the master of metaphysics and "Pictor Optimus", as they called him, lived the last thirty years of his life, together with his second wife, Isabella. The house is now a foundation devoted to the safeguarding and promotion of De Chirico's oeuvre. Visiting offers a glimpse into the artist's private and everyday world. On display is a collection of historical works, such as *The Prodigal Son*, *Orpheus the Tired Troubador*, and *The Return of Ulysses*, as well as later works like *The Three Graces* (1954), after the painting by Peter Paul Rubens. Also on view are priceless works of art inspired by the paintings of some of the world's masters.

"THEY SAY THAT ROME IS AT THE CENTER OF THE WORLD AND THAT PIAZZA DI SPAGNA IS IN THE CENTER OF ROME, THEREFORE, MY WIFE AND I, WOULD INDEED BE LIVING IN THE CENTER OF THE WORLD, WHICH WOULD BE THE APEX OF CENTRALITY, AND THE APOGEE OF ANTI-ECCENTRICITY."
GIORGIO DE CHIRICO

piazza di Spagna 31
+39 06 679 65 46
reservations required on website
fondazionedechirico.org

EATING TIP
NINO DAL 1934
via Borgognona 11
+39 06 678 67 52
ristorantenino.it
open 12:30-3 p.m.
and 7:30-11 p.m.
closed Sun

 2 MINUTES

DE CHIRICO AT THE GNAM

The Galleria Nazionale d'Arte Moderna (GNAM; National Gallery of Modern Art) houses an important core of works by Giorgio de Chirico in Room 38, which is entirely devoted to the master. This invaluable collection shows how the artist's research evolved over his lifetime. On display are, among others, *Lucretia*, 1922; *The Pregnant Woman* (copy after Raphael), 1923; *Portrait of the Artist's Mother*, 1911; *Horseman with a Red Cap and Blue Cloak*, 1939; *Mysterious Spectacle*, 1971; *Return to the Castle*, 1969; *Self-Portrait with Head of Minerva*, 1958; *The Disquieting Muses*, 1925; *Angelica and Ruggero*, 1946; *The Tower of Silence*, 1937; *The Tower and the Train*, 1934; and *Still Life with Fish*, 1925.

A STONE'S THROW AWAY IS THE JAPANESE INSTITUTE, WHICH HAS A LOVELY SEN'EN-STYLE GARDEN (GARDEN WITH A LAKE) CREATED IN THE 1960s. FOR FURTHER INFORMATION, VISIT JFROMA.IT.

viale delle Belle Arti 131
+39 06 322 981
open 8:30 a.m.-7:30 p.m., closed Mon
gnam.beniculturali.it

EATING TIP
CAFFÈ DELLE ARTI
Galleria Nazionale
d'Arte Moderna
via Antonio Gramsci 73
+39 06 326 51 236
caffedelleartiroma.com
open 8 a.m.-midnight
Mon 8 a.m.-5 p.m.

 2 MINUTES

FORO ITALICO

Inaugurated in 1932 under the name Foro Mussolini, the Foro Italico, a vast sports facility designed and built between 1927 and 1938 according to a design by Enrico Del Debbio and Luigi Moretti, was completed after the Second World War. Monumental and based on perfect symmetries, the Foro Italico is one of the major examples of Rationalist architecture, at the same time preserving a rarefied atmosphere that alludes to the Metaphysical settings in the paintings of Giorgio de Chirico. The facility was conceived to celebrate the cult of the body and sports promoted by fascism: the most evident example is the Stadium of Marbles, embellished with colossal and impressive statues of athletes inspired by models from Classical Antiquity, almost an open-air museum of early twentieth-century Italian sculpture. The Grande Piazzale dell'Impero instead celebrates the regime's political success, visible in the black and white tile mosaic floor. Among the other structures of the facility are the Academy of Physical Education and the buildings designed by Costantino Costantini: the Baths, the Academy of Music, the Tennis Stadium, the Monolith, and one of the guest quarters.

viale del Foro Italico

THE WALK OF FAME, HONORING LEGENDS OF ITALIAN SPORTS, WAS INAUGURATED ON VIALE DELLE OLIMPIADI IN 2015. IT CONSISTS OF 100 BRICKS BEARING THE NAMES OF ITALIAN ATHLETES AND THE SYMBOL OF THE SPORT THEY PLAYED.

EATING TIP
CUCCURUCÙ
via Capoprati 10
+39 06 375 18 558
cuccurucu.info
open 12:30-3 p.m.
and 7:30 p.m.-midnight

 12 MINUTES

Museo Carlo Bilotti

Located in the Orangerie of the Villa Borghese, in the heart of Rome's greenest area, is the Museo Carlo Bilotti, named after the Cosenza-born collector and patron of the arts who traveled the world. Bilotti donated to the city of Rome his collection of eighteen paintings, sculptures, and watercolors by Giorgio de Chirico (the sculpture *Hector and Andromache* stands outside the museum), as well as works by Andy Warhol, Roy Lichtenstein, Salvador Dalí, Niki de Saint-Phalle, Mimmo Rotella, Gino Severini, and Giacomo Manzù.

Continuing along Via dell'Aranciera, visitors will find the spectacular garden of the lake. Located on an artificial island is an Ionic-style temple dedicated to Asclepius. It was built in 1786 by Antonio and Mario Asprucci, and by Cristoforo Unterperger.

viale Fiorello La Guardia 6
+39 06 06 08
winter 10 a.m.-4 p.m., Sat-Sun 10 a.m.-7 p.m., closed Mon
summer 1-7 p.m., Sat-Sun 10 a.m.-7 p.m., closed Mon
www.museocarlobilotti.it

Eating Tip
Harry's Bar
via Vittorio Veneto 150
+39 06 484 643
harrysbar.it
open 10 a.m.-2 p.m.

 9 MINUTES

Palazzo dei Congressi – Eur

The Palazzo dei Ricevimenti e dei Congressi (Reception and Congress Building) in the EUR district was designed by the architect Adalberto Libera in 1938. Together with the Palazzo della Civiltà Italiana, it is one of the finest examples of Italian Rationalist style. Combining modernity and classicism, it contains works by major twentieth-century artists. In 1953 Gino Severini, a leading figure in the Futurist movement, produced 180 feet of decorative panels on the theme of agriculture for the building; Achille Funi produced a fresco on the origins of Rome; and Angelo Canevari is the author of the mosaics decorating the room currently used as a cafeteria. Of particular interest is the hanging open-air theater, which is entirely made of Carrara marble and has a stage that measures 8,008 square feet.

piazza John Fitzgerald Kennedy 1
+39 06 545 13 710

Eating Tip
TATÀ
piazza Guglielmo Marconi 11
+39 06 592 01 05
ristopizzeriatata.it
open 12-3:30 p.m.
and 7:30 p.m.-midnight

 1 MINUTE

Palazzo della Civiltà Italiana – EUR

The majestic Palazzo della Civiltà Italiana is considered the architectural icon of twentieth-century Rome. Designed in 1937 by Giovanni Guerrini, Ernesto Bruno La Padula, and Mario Romano, it was intended as the fulcrum of the 1942 World Exhibition. The building is an example of the fusion between classical Roman architecture and the principles of Rationalism. It is the stylized version of the famous arches of the Flavian Amphitheater, celebrating the myth of the re-emergence of the Roman Empire. This is also where it gets its name, "Colosseo Quadrato." The 28 statues on the ground floor, each of which represent a typical national trade or talent, and the inscription on each side of the building, "A people of poets, artists, saints, thinkers, scientists, sailors, and explorers," are a tribute to the gifts of the Italian people. Today, the building is a deep-rooted symbol brimming with meaning, which will continue to write its own history, merging tradition and innovation. It is precisely the idea of sharing these values that persuaded FENDI, in 2015, to choose this building as its general headquarters, breathing new life into it with an exhibition space open to the public, a tribute to creativity, design, art, and to the artisanship of the Made in Italy brand.

Quadrato della Concordia 3
+39 06 334 501

Among the many films in which what is known as the "square Colosseum" was used as a setting are *Rome, Open City* (1945) by Roberto Rossellini; *The Eclipse* (1962) by Michelangelo Antonioni; *8 1/2* (1963) by Federico Fellini; *The Belly of an Architect*, (1987) by Peter Greenaway; and *Witches to the North* (2001) by Giovanni Veronesi.

EATING TIP
CAFFÈ PALOMBINI
piazzale K. Adenauer 12
+39 06 591 17 00
palombini.com
Mon Tue Wed Thur
7 a.m.-10 p.m.
Fri Sat 7 a.m.-1 p.m.
Sun 8 a.m.-10 p.m.

 3 MINUTES

. Playlist .

"FINDER"
Moderat

"PHOBOS"
Rodion

"BEARSONG"
Hess Is More

"PIANO BEAT"
Flavia Lazzarini

"GO"
The Chemical Brothers

"HI & LOW"
WhoMadeWho

"PREBEN GOES TO ACAPULCO"
Todd Terje

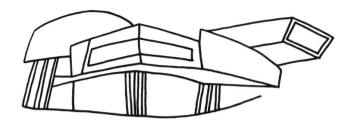

CONTEMPORARY ROME

R ome is commonly, and perhaps naturally, associated with Antiquity because of the huge artistic and architectural heritage of which it is a sovereign guardian. In the midst of tradition and history the focus of creativity has never dwindled, and the spirit of modernity and exploration, since the late nineteenth century, has stimulated artistic life in the city. Here are seven institutional spaces addressed to the contemporary: museums, but also galleries and private foundations that guarantee for Rome an ongoing conversation with the international scenario and that are often works in themselves.

Casino dei Principi and the Roman School

Housed inside the elegant architectural complex of Villa Torlonia are examples of Roman art from the late nineteenth and early twentieth centuries. The Casino Nobile, with its ornamentation and original decor, hosts a small museum with a collection of antique and Neoclassical works that belonged to the Torlonia family, as well as a priceless collection of works by the Roman School. This movement was affirmed in the interwar period through such illustrious figures as Mafai, Raphaël, Donghi, Cagli, Leoncillo, Trombadori, Basaldella, Fazzini, Pirandello, Capogrossi, and Vespignani, among many others. In 1983 the Archivio della Scuola Romana was founded in the Casino dei Principi, where temporary exhibitions are held. Also founded was the Museo della Casina delle Civette, a space dedicated to glass art, a genre that developed in Rome in the early twentieth century from the collaboration between the great Roman glassworker Cesare Picchiarini and artists like Duilio Cambellotti, Umberto Bottazzi, and Paolo Paschetto.

via Nomentana 70
+39 06 06 08
open 9 a.m.-7 p.m., closed Mon
museivillatorlonia.it

EATING TIP
RISTORANTE
ELEONORA D'ARBOREA
corso Trieste 23
+39 06 442 50 943
ristoranteeleonoradarborea.com
open 12:30-3:30 p.m.
and 7:30-11:30 p.m.
closed Mon

 5 MINUTES

Galleria d'Arte Moderna

The Modern Art Gallery on Via Crispi houses perhaps the most complete collection of Italian artworks, from the post-Risorgimento period to the Second World War; on view are examples of the major artistic currents that once dialogued with the European avant-gardes. Founded in 1925 and considerably enriched from the 1930s onward, the gallery now numbers some 3,000 works, including masterpieces by Vincenzo Gemito, Nino Costa, Adolfo De Carolis, Antonio Donghi, Giorgio de Chirico, Mario Mafai, Scipione, Gino Severini, Giacomo Balla, Felice Casorati, Giorgio Morandi, Giuseppe Capogrossi, Afro, Alberto Savinio, Carlo Carrà, Mario Sironi, and Renato Guttuso; sculptors include Arturo Martini, Marino Marini, and Giacomo Manzù. Since 1995 the gallery has been located in the ancient monastery of the Carmelitane Scalze (Discalced Carmelites), where works from the collections are exhibited on a rotating basis; also organized are temporary shows, surrounded by the carefully thought-out museum spaces.

via Francesco Crispi 24
+39 06 474 29 04
open 10 a.m.-6:30 p.m., closed Mon
galleriaartemodernaroma.it

In addition, the Modern Art Gallery offers permanent tactile experiences to the visually impaired. The glass cloister houses a selection of sculptures, accompanied by information that prepares visitors for their tour.

EATING TIP
ENOTECA
BUCCONE
via di Ripetta 19/20
+39 06 361 21 54
www.enotecabuccone.com
Mon-Thur 9 a.m.-8:30 p.m.
Fri-Sat 9 a.m.-11:30 p.m.
Sun 11 a.m.-7 p.m.

 6 MINUTES

GNAM - GALLERIA NAZIONALE D'ARTE MODERNA

A temple of modern and contemporary
art, since 1883 the GNAM has gathered an
immense collection of works that tells the
history of Italy. Many of its newest acquisitions
come from the national exhibitions and the
Venice Biennale: Verism, Symbolism, Neo-
Renaissance Decadentism, the Secessions, the
avant-garde, and more. It also houses works by
Mondrian, Pollock, Modigliani, Moore, Burri,
Colla, Capogrossi, Fontana, and Manzoni,
as well as kinetic art and programmed art.
The GNAM is a must-see for art lovers and
those who would like to learn more about the
principal art movements in one of Italy's largest
collections of twentieth-century art.

EATING TIP
CAFFÈ DELLE ARTI
Galleria Nazionale
d'Arte Moderna
via Antonio Gramsci 73
+39 06 326 51 236
caffedelleartiroma.com
open 8 a.m.-midnight
Mon 8 a.m.-5 p.m.

🚶 2 MINUTES

viale delle Belle Arti 131
+39 06 322 981
open 8:30 a.m.-7:30 p.m., closed Mon
gnam.beniculturali.it

MACRO TESTACCIO

The MACRO Testaccio, one of the two locations of the Museo d'Arte Contemporanea in Rome (the other one is on Via Nizza), hovers aesthetically between classicism and modernity. Formerly the city's slaughterhouse, it was repurposed in the late nineteenth century to a design by the architect Gioacchino Ersoch. Its earlier pavilions are an important example of late twentieth-century industrial architecture. Since 2002, two more pavilions have been added, thus turning the venue into a huge concept space used for exhibitions, teaching, and laboratory activities, all within the heart of working-class Rome.

THE TESTACCIO, OR "MOUNTAIN OF POTTERY" (CALLED *TESTAE* IN LATIN), GETS ITS NAME FROM THE PLACE WHERE TERRACOTTA VESSELS WERE DISCARDED DURING THE ROMAN AGE. AFTER BEING UNLOADED AT THE RIVER PORT OF THE EMPORIUM (NO LONGER EXTANT) AND HAVING THEIR CONTENTS REMOVED, THE CERAMIC WARES WERE BROKEN UP AND STACKED TO CREATE THE ARTIFICIAL TESTACCIO HILL, CURRENTLY 115 FEET HIGH, FOR A SURFACE AREA OF 215,000 SQUARE FEET.

EATING TIP
MORDI E VAI
Via Franklin 12 E
Nuovo mercato Testaccio
Box 15
mordievai.it
open 8 a.m.-2:30 p.m.
closed Sun

 2 MINUTES

piazza Orazio Giustiniani 4
+39 06 06 08
open 2-8 p.m., closed Mon
(open only for exhibitions)
museomacro.org

MACRO VIA NIZZA

A visit to the main branch of the Museum of Contemporary Art of the City of Rome is a journey into the heart of the city in movement. Made from what was formerly the Birra Peroni brewery building in the Salario-Nomentano quarter, this is a magnificent example of industrial archaeology. It was designed by the French architect Odile Decq, whose idea was to create a place characterized by a rhythmical red and black motif. A visit to the museum is a unique experience and an introduction to contemporary art through its many temporary events, conferences, workshops, and the collection of works by Roman artists from different generations, ranging from the early twentieth-century masters to artists from the 1980s and 1990s to the most recent generation of emerging artists, including representatives of street art.

NOT FAR FROM HERE IS PORTA PIA (1561), THE GATE DEDICATED TO PIUS IV, ALSO KNOWN AS THE BARBER POPE. IT APPEARS THAT THE POPE DESCENDED FROM A MILANESE FAMILY OF BARBERS, DESPITE THE FACT THAT THEY BOASTED THEIR DESCENT FROM THE MEDICIS. MICHELANGELO BUONARROTI DECORATED THE DOOR IN A HIGHLY ORIGINAL WAY—IF YOU LOOK AT IT FROM VIA XX SETTEMBRE, YOU'LL SEE A BARBER'S BOWL, SOAP, AND TOWELS.

via Nizza 138
+39 06 671 070 400
open 10:30 a.m.-7:30 p.m., closed Mon
museomacro.org

EATING TIP
IL VIAGGIO
via Isonzo 14
+39 06 979 97 043
ristoranteilviaggio.it
open 12:30-3 p.m.
and 7-11 p.m.
Sat 7-11 p.m.
Sun 12:30-3 p.m.

 6 MINUTES

MAXXI

A visit to this museum dedicated to twenty-first-century arts—art, architecture, and design—is a must for anyone wishing to learn about the international art scene from inside one of the masterpieces of postmodern architecture. Designed by the Iranian architect Zaha Hadid and officially opened in 2010, the MAXXI is a magical interweaving of solid volumes and liquid walkways, curvilinear walls and deep voids letting in the natural light. As well as the temporary exhibitions, visitors can see a collection of works by contemporary masters such as Alighiero Boetti, Francesco Clemente, William Kentridge, Mario Merz, Gerhard Richter, Anish Kapoor, Carlo Scarpa, Maurizio Sacripanti, and Aldo Rossi, among others.

HELD EVERY YEAR AT MAXXI, YAP (YOUNG ARCHITECTS PROGRAM) PROMOTES AND SUPPORTS EMERGING ARCHITECTURAL TALENT AND IS ORGANIZED IN COLLABORATION WITH THE MUSEUM OF MODERN ART AND MOMA PS1 IN NEW YORK CITY; CONSTRUCTO, BASED IN SANTIAGO DE CHILE; ISTANBUL MODERN; AND THE MMCA (NATIONAL MUSEUM OF MODERN AND CONTEMPORARY ART) IN SEOUL.

via Guido Reni 4
+39 06 322 51 78
open 11 a.m.-7 p.m., Sat 11 a.m.-11 p.m.,
closed Mon
fondazionemaxxi.it

EATING TIP
TIEPOLO
- BOTTIGLIERIA
BISTROT
via Giovanni Battista
Tiepolo 3
+39 06 322 74 49
open 1 p.m.-2 a.m.

 9 MINUTES

PALAZZO DELLE ESPOSIZIONI

The Palazzo delle Esposizioni is an events space in which exhibitions in all the arts are organized: fine art, cinema, theater, architecture, and photography are presented within this Neoclassical building. After years of restoration and adaptive reuse the PalaExpo has become Rome's largest interdisciplinary exhibition space, with over 10,000 square meters renovated using advanced technology and materials in a bioclimatic approach. It has a room where movies can be screened as well as a rooftop restaurant, the Open Colonna (one Michelin star), for creative dinners with a view of Rome.

"I AM FOR AN ART THAT EMBROILS ITSELF WITH THE EVERYDAY CRAP AND STILL COMES OUT ON TOP.
I AM FOR THE ART THAT A KID LICKS, AFTER PEELING AWAY THE WRAPPER."

CLAES OLDENBURG

EATING TIP
OPEN COLONNA
via Milano 9A
+39 06 478 22 641
antonellocolonna.it/open
Tue Wed Thur Fri Sat
12:30-3:30 p.m. and
8-11 p.m.
Sun and Mon
12:30-3:30 p.m.
🏃 2 MINUTES

via Nazionale 194
+39 06 399 67 500
open 10 a.m.-8 p.m., Fri-Sat 10 a.m.-10:30 p.m., closed Mon
palazzoesposizioni.it

GALLERIES
AND FOUNDATIONS

●

Contributing to the cultural fervor of the city's contemporary art institutions are its galleries, foundations, and, of course, the artists. Rome has always been famous for its galleries, which serve as a link between the city and international art. This ongoing tradition has been sustained by the exhibitions, teaching programs, and various projects involving individuals and their private spaces. Such initiatives constantly introduce and support new talents, whether Italian or foreign, promoting them locally and on the international market and working hard to make the most significant names in Italian art known to the rest of the world.

Fondazione Giuliani
via Gustavo Bianchi 1
+39 06 573 01 091
www.fondazionegiuliani.org

Fondazione Memmo
via della Fontanella
di Borghese 56
+39 06 681 36 598
fondazionememmo.it

Fondazione Pastificio Cerere
via degli Ausoni 1
+39 06 454 22 960
pastificiocerere.it

Gagosian Gallery
via Francesco Crispi 16
+39 06 420 86 498
gagosian.com

Galleria 1/9
via degli Specchi 20
+39 06 976 13 696
unosunove.com

Galleria Lorcan O'Neill
vicolo dei Catinari 3
+39 06 688 92 980
lorcanoneill.com

Galleria Marie-Laure Fleisch
via di Pallacorda 15
+39 06 688 91 936
galleriamlf.com

Galleria T293
via Giovanni Mario Crescimbeni 11
+39 06 889 80 475
t293.it

Galleria Valentina Bonomo
via del Portico d'Ottavia 13
+39 06 683 27 66
galleriabonomo.com

Giustini / Stagetti Galleria O. Roma
via dell'Arancio 46/49
+39 06 897 60 540
giustinistagetti.com

Indipendenza Studio
via dei Mille 6
+39 06 447 03 249
indipendenzastudio.com

Magazzino
via dei Prefetti 17
+39 06 687 59 51
magazzinoartemoderna.com

Monitor Gallery
via Sforza Cesarini 43
+39 06 393 78 024
monitoronline.org

Nomas Foundation
viale Somalia 33
+39 06 863 98 381
nomasfoundation.com

**Quadriennale di Roma
Villa Carpegna**
circonvallazione
Aurelia 72
+39 06 977 45 31
quadriennalediroma.org

Studio Sales
piazza Dante 2
+39 06 775 91 122
studiosales.it

The Gallery Apart
via Francesco Negri 43
+39 06 688 09 863
thegalleryapart.it

THE BUILDINGS OF POWER

This tour will accompany you to the heart of governmental and administrative Rome. The historic buildings that host the nerve centers of Italian politics are filled with some surprising masterpieces, which visitors can only view on rare occasions when the buildings are open to the public, however. Visitors should check in advance to find out if special openings are scheduled. Owing to their majesty and architectural beauty, these buildings with their impressive facades are in any case well worth seeing from the outside. You can always try looking beyond the entrance door to catch a glimpse of the inner courtyards, or through a window to see any one of the details in the richly decorated ceilings.

. PLAYLIST .

"CONVERSAZIONE"
Mina

"ZENITH"
Soulstance

"DANCE ME TO THE END OF LOVE"
Madeleine Peyroux

"FRÉNÉSIE"
René Aubry

"INTRASPETTRO"
Les Hommes

"L-O-V-E"
Nat King Cole

"FEELING GOOD"
Nina Simone

CURIA IULIA, FORO ROMANO

At the end of the short side of the Foro Romano (Roman Forum), behind Piazza Venezia, is a large brick building called Curia Julia (Curia Iulia); it was completed and inaugurated by Emperor Augustus on August 28 in 29 BC. This ancient seat of the Roman Senate is a tall building, probably because it needed to have good acoustics. It is divided into three sections, with three wide, low steps to either side. The approximately 300 seats of the *curiati* (that is, the senators who made up the chief council of state) were at one time located here. Near the Curia look for the *Lacus Curtius*, once the site of a mysterious widening chasm. Livy wrote that for Rome to overcome a peril it was facing, it had to throw in that which it held dearest. Marcus Curtius believed that the Romans most cherished the life of one of their brave youths, so he plunged into the opening on his horse, and the chasm closed up forever.

via dei Fori Imperiali
+39 06 06 08
open 8:30 a.m. until 2 hours before sunset
archeoroma.beniculturali.it

EATING TIP
LA TAVERNA DEI FORI IMPERIALI
via della Madonna dei Monti 9
+39 06 679 86 43
open 12:30-3 p.m. and 7:30-10:30 p.m.
closed Tue

 3 MINUTES

FARNESINA

The headquarters of the Ministry of Foreign Affairs and International Cooperation owes its name to the land that once belonged to the Farnese family, on which it was built to a design by the architects Enrico Del Debbio, Arnaldo Foschini, and Vittorio Ballio Morpurgo. One of the finest examples of Italian Rationalist architecture, the Farnesina has 1,320 rooms and a facade measuring over 1,800 square feet, making it one of Italy's largest buildings. The Farnesina Porte Aperte (Farnesina Doors Open) program offers visitors a chance to see the building and its rich collection of modern and contemporary art.

ONE OF THE SYMBOLS OF THE FARNESINA IS THE BRONZE SPHERE BY THE ARTIST ARNALDO POMODORO, WHICH STANDS OUT AT THE CENTER OF THE FOUNTAIN IN THE SQUARE: IT IS A PERFECTLY SMOOTH SPHERE WITH A CRACK IN IT THAT LETS US GLIMPSE THE COMPLEX MECHANISM INSIDE. INTERPRET IT AS YOU WISH.

EATING TIP
IL QUINTO QUARTO
via della Farnesina 13
+39 06 333 87 68
ilquintoquarto.it
open 8.p m.-1 a.m.
closed Sun

piazzale della Farnesina 1
+39 06 369 11
esteri.it

 11 MINUTES

MONTECITORIO

This impressive palazzo is the heart of the Republic of Italy because it is the seat of the Chamber of Deputies. Pope Innocent X commissioned Gian Lorenzo Bernini to design the building, which was later completed by Carlo Fontana, who added the bell gable and two doors to the sides of the main entrance. An expansion of the building in the twentieth century was commissioned from Ernesto Basile, who also designed the debate chamber and the great "Corridor of Lost Steps," also known as the "Transatlantico." This elegant salon in Italian Liberty style, in which the deputies can relax between parliamentary sessions, is open to visitors the first Sunday of the month.

MONTECITORIO HAS A HUGE ART COLLECTION THAT INCLUDES ARCHAEOLOGICAL FINDS, JEWELRY, TAPESTRIES, BUSTS, AND ABOUT A THOUSAND PAINTINGS DATED BETWEEN THE SIXTEENTH AND TWENTIETH CENTURIES, AS WELL AS SEVERAL THOUSAND ENGRAVINGS AND PRINTS FROM VARIOUS PERIODS.

EATING TIP
ZUMA
Palazzo FENDI
via della Fontanella
di Borghese 48
+39 06 992 66 622
zumarestaurant.com
open 12-3 p.m.
and 7-11:30 p.m.
closed Mon
🚶 5 MINUTES

piazza di Monte Citorio,
camera.it

Palazzo Chigi

Palazzo Chigi is located on Via del Corso in Piazza Colonna, just a stone's throw from Montecitorio. Since 1961 it has been the seat of Italian government and the prime minister's official residence. Built in the sixteenth century and for many years the private residence of the Roman nobility, it was acquired by the state in 1916. The impressive stairway known as the *Scalone d'onore* is decorated with the Chigi family coat of arms, antique statuary, Roman sarcophagi, and seventeenth-century bronze lanterns. To visit the palace you need to book one of the guided tours available from October to May every Saturday morning (from 9 a.m. to 12 p.m.). The tours, which last about an hour and are free, follow a planned route.

THE BALCONY ON THE CORNER OF VIA DEL CORSO AND PIAZZA COLONNA IS KNOWN AS THE "BOW OF ITALY," FOR IT WAS FROM HERE THAT BENITO MUSSOLINI GAVE HIS FIRST SPEECHES IN 1922.

EATING TIP
TRATTORIA DAL CAVALIER GINO
vicolo Rosini 4
+39 06 687 34 34
open 1-2:30 p.m.
and 8-10:30 p.m.
closed Sun

🚶 4 MINUTES

piazza Colonna 370
governo.it

Palazzo Madama

A must when visiting the heart of the capital is the seat of the Italian Senate, located between Piazza Navona and the Pantheon. Construction began in the late fifteenth century and was completed according to a design by Giuliano da Sangallo after the building was acquired by the Medici family. It owes its name to two women who, in different periods, spent long sojourns here: Madama Margaret of Austria and Violante Beatrice of Bavaria, Gian Gastone de' Medici's sister-in-law. Palazzo Madama also has a rich art collection. If you want to visit the palace, be sure to check the calendar; tours are free and usually held on the first Saturday of each month.

In the eighteenth century, when Palazzo Madama was transferred from the Medici family to the Papal State, it was used as a police headquarters. Hence, the expression in dialect "la Madama," which the Romans to this day still use to refer to the police.

Eating Tip
QUE TE PONGO
SALMONERIA
via della Dogana
Vecchia 13
+39 06 688 03 029
open 9 a.m.-8 p.m.
closed Sun

 2 MINUTES

piazza Madama
+ 39 06 670 62 177
senato.it

Quirinal Palace

Inside this palace is where the president of the Italian Republic lives, and so it has also come to symbolize the Italian state. Also known as "the Hill" (from Collis Quirinalis, the name of the hill on which it is located), the Quirinal Palace was built in the late sixteenth century. Over the centuries, its 1,200 rooms have hosted popes, kings, and other dignitaries; since 1946, when the republic was proclaimed, it has served as the official residence of Italy's president. Concerts and exhibitions, as well as the many tours given here, make this a place close to the heart of the Italian people.
For those wishing to visit the palace, reservations should be made at least five days in advance.

THE SALONE DELLE FESTE IS THE PALACE'S LARGEST, MOST SOLEMN ROOM. THIS IS WHERE THE GOVERNMENT IS SWORN IN AND OFFICIAL DINNERS FOR HEADS OF STATE ARE HELD. THE FLOOR IS FITTED WITH WHAT IS THOUGHT TO BE THE SECOND LARGEST CARPET IN THE WORLD, MEASURING JUST UNDER 300 SQUARE METERS.

EATING TIP
PICCOLO ARANCIO
vicolo Scanderberg 112
+39 06 678 61 39
open 12-3 p.m. and
7-midnight
closed Mon

🚶 4 MINUTES

piazza del Quirinale
+39 06 399 67 557
palazzo.quirinale.it

Fountains
and Holy Water

Rome and water have been related for centuries. The ancient Romans were already using surprisingly advanced engineering techniques to build not only the aqueducts that supplied the containers and artificial basins used by the empire's many citizens but also those marvelous works of urban architecture: fountains. Indeed, the Italian capital has over 2,000 fountains of various types: hemicycle, cascade, groin, facade, grotto, and the termini of aqueducts, as well as countless troughs, drinking fountains, and so-called *nasoni* (big noses). Visitors will be awed by the creations of Italy's masters of art and architecture, which triumph in squares that are almost hidden by the intricate, labyrinthine pattern of streets and alleyways.

· PLAYLIST ·

"FONTANA DI TREVI"
Katyna Ranieri

"TEMPTATION & SEDUCTION"
Jen

"SPRUCE"
Dusky

"FOUNTAIN"
Iamamiwhoami

"CLUB NINE"
Nicolas Godin

"SUNSCAPE"
Jfc

"MISS YOU"
Trentemøller

Fontana dei Dioscuri

This fountain, located in the center of Piazza del Quirinale, is protected by the majestic statues of the Dioscuri, Castor and Pollux, who hold their horses by the reins. After several restorations, the original basin was dismantled and replaced by a circular one made of granite that had been found in the Campo Vaccino area of the Roman Forum, once a cattle trough in the forum's Roman period. The fountain's obelisk is one of thirteen found in Rome; it stands over 46 feet tall and was made in Egypt of red granite from Aswan, then transported to Rome in the first century AD.

No other city in the world has as many obelisks; Rome also holds the record for the tallest one—the obelisk of San Giovanni in Laterano, at more than 104 feet tall.

EATING TIP
MATERMATUTA
via Milano 48/50
+39 06 482 39 62
matermatuta.eu
open 1-3 p.m.
and 7:30-11:30 p.m.
closed Sun

🚶 6 MINUTES

piazza del Quirinale
palazzo.quirinale.it

Fontana dei Quattro Fiumi

Since the day it was unveiled on June 12, 1651, the Fountain of the Four Rivers, a spectacular example of Baroque sculpture by Gian Lorenzo Bernini, has aroused wonder and awe, as chronicles from the past tell us. This complex and highly articulated group of marble figures personifies the Nile, the Plate, the Ganges, and the Danube. Located at the center of Piazza Navona over the place where the Stadium of Domitian stood during the Roman age, the sculptural group supports, in a scene characterized by intense movement, an Egyptian obelisk made of granite at the top of which is a dove, the symbol of the Holy Spirit and the pope who commissioned it, Innocent X.

LEGEND SAYS THAT THE NILE'S VEILED HEAD CONVEYS BERNINI'S DISLIKE FOR THE NEARBY CHURCH DESIGNED BY BORROMINI, WHILE THE PLATE, CRINGING WITH ARM UPRAISED, IS SUPPOSED TO EXPRESS BERNINI'S FEAR THAT THE CHURCH WILL COLLAPSE. HOWEVER, THESE STORIES HAVE NO BASIS IN FACT. BERNINI HAD COMPLETED THE FOUNTAIN A YEAR BEFORE BORROMINI STARTED WORKING ON THE CHURCH.

EATING TIP
IL SANLORENZO
via dei Chiavari 4/5
+39 06 686 50 97
ilsanlorenzo.it
Sat & Mon 7:30-11:45 p.m.
Tue Wed Thur Fri
12:45- 2:45 p.m.
and 7:30-11:45 p.m.
closed Sun
🚶 7 MINUTES

piazza Navona

Fontana dell'Acqua Paola

Overlooking a breathtaking view of the Janiculum, this monumental fountain was built to celebrate the restoration of the Trajan aqueduct that Pope Paul V (born Camillo Borghese) had built in the seventeenth century. The Romans affectionately call it "er fontanone," and it was inspired by the triumphal arches of ancient Rome, its facade characterized by five arches and six imposing marble columns. The entire work is embellished with the coat of arms of the Borghese family, characterized by dragons and eagles, which also adorn the pillars around the large pool of water.

THE FONTANA DELL'ACQUA PAOLA IS A STUNNING BACKDROP; PAOLO SORRENTINO CHOSE IT FOR ONE OF THE FIRST SCENES OF THE OSCAR-WINNING MOVIE *THE GREAT BEAUTY* (2013).

EATING TIP
ANTICO ARCO
piazzale Aurelio 7
+39 06 581 52 74
anticoarco.it
open noon-midnight

🚶 6 MINUTES

via Garibaldi al Gianicolo

Fontana
delle Tartarughe

This complex and elegant composition in bronze and marble, made according to a design by Giacomo Della Porta, is rich in decorative elements related to water: dolphins, shells, and, of course, tortoises (*tartarughe*), which were made by Gian Lorenzo Bernini and added when the fountain was restored. Legend has it that Duke Mattei had the fountain built overnight as a surprise for his future bride.

ORIGINALLY, THE FOUR EPHEBES WERE INTENDED TO SUPPORT DOLPHINS THAT SPOUTED, BUT THERE WAS NOT ENOUGH WATER PRESSURE TO ACHIEVE THE DESIRED EFFECT, SO THE DOLPHINS WERE REPLACED. BERNINI'S ORIGINAL TORTOISES WERE STOLEN IN 1944; THREE WERE EVENTUALLY FOUND AND ARE NOW ON DISPLAY AT THE CAPITOLINE MUSEUMS. THOSE ON THE FOUNTAIN ARE COPIES.

EATING TIP
GIGGETTO AL PORTICO D'OTTAVIA
via del Portico d'Ottavia 21
+39 06 686 11 05
giggetto.it
open 12:30-3 p.m.
and 7:30-11 p.m.
closed Mon

🚶 2 MINUTES

piazza Mattei

FONTANA DI TREVI

No doubt one of the jewels of the Eternal City, an absolute triumph in Late Roman Baroque style, is the Trevi Fountain (1735), commissioned by Pope Clement XII from Nicola Salvi. The fountain rises up behind Palazzo Poli and is the most successful example of fusion between architecture and sculpture. The exuberant and scenographic composition and decoration, focusing specifically on the figure of Ocean and generally on the theme of the sea and water's symbolic value, have forever been a source of inspiration for poets, artists, and musicians. The fountain has also been used as a spectacular setting for countless movies, perhaps the most famous being Federico Fellini's *La Dolce Vita* (1960), in which the fountain is a veritable protagonist alongside Anita Ekberg and Marcello Mastroianni. Anyone who hopes to return to Rome must engage in the popular ritual of tossing a coin into its waters while making a wish. The fountain was brought back to its ancient splendor in 2015 thanks to the restoration work funded by FENDI as part of the FENDI for Fountains project, dedicated to safeguarding the city's historical monuments and attractions. Restoration of the fountains of the Gianicolo, the Mosè, the Ninfeo del Pincio, and the aqueduct of the Peschiera is scheduled for the coming years.

piazza di Trevi

EATING TIP
TRATTORIA
AL MORO
vicolo delle Bollette 13
+39 06 678 34 95
ristorantealmororoma.com
open 1-3:30 p.m.
and 8-11:30 p.m.
closed Sun

🚶 2 MINUTES

FONTANA DI VILLA MEDICI

Commissioned by Cardinal Ferdinand de' Medici and built in the late sixteenth century, this fountain consists of a large octagonal basin, a gray granite bowl, and a marble ball with spurting water that, as legend has it, replaced the original lily, symbol of the Medici dynasty. The legend recounting the origin of this ball is unique: it seems that Queen Christina of Sweden, famous for her eccentric personality, was late for an appointment at Villa Medici, so to let her hosts know she hadn't forgotten, she asked that a cannonball be shot from the terrace of Castel Sant'Angelo. That very cannonball now decorates the fountain, which is why it is called the Cannonball Fountain.

CLEARLY VISIBLE ON THE BRONZE DOOR TO THE VILLA MEDICI IS A ROUND MARK. COULD IT HAVE BEEN LEFT BY THE CANNONBALL CHRISTINA HAD LAUNCHED FROM CASTEL SANT'ANGELO?

EATING TIP
RISTORANTE ATELIER CANOVA TADOLINI
via del Babuino 150/A
+39 06 321 10 702
canovatadolini.com
open 8 a.m.-midnight

🏃 7 MINUTES

piazza della Trinità dei Monti 1

Quattro Fontane

A wonderful surprise awaits you at the intersection of the Via delle Quattro Fontane and the Via del Quirinale. At the corners of the buildings are four semicircular travertine basins topped by niches framing four allegorical figures: two males, the Tiber and the Arno, and two females, Diana and Juno, symbolizing Strength and Fidelity, because they each hold a lion and a dog, respectively. Visitors will be captivated by the fine detail in the background. This complex work by the sculptor Domenico Fontana was made between 1588 and 1593; it was restored in 2015, together with the Trevi Fountain, as part of the FENDI for Fountains project, dedicated to safeguarding the city's historical monuments and famous sights. Restoration of the fountains of the Gianicolo, the Mosè, the Ninfeo del Pincio, and of the aqueduct of the Peschiera has also been scheduled for 2016.

STANDING OVER THE ARNO FOUNTAIN, ON THE CORNER OF VIA XX SETTEMBRE, IS THE PALAZZO ALBANI DEL DRAGO. THE LIBRARY OF CARDINAL ALBANI, AN EXPERT BIBLIOPHILE, NUMBERS AS MANY AS 40,000 VOLUMES. THE GROUND FLOOR ONCE HOSTED A PRIVATE THEATER, KNOWN AS THE TEATRO DELLE QUATTRO FONTANE, WHICH WAS ACTIVE UNTIL 1914.

EATING TIP
RISTORANTE ZEUS
via Nazionale 251/A
+39 06 489 05 444
ristorantezeus.com
open noon-midnight

🚶 5 MINUTES

via delle Quattro Fontane
corner of via del Quirinale

. Playlist .

"ANCORA TU"
Róisín Murphy

"TAKI RARI"
Yma Sumac

"UNE VERY STYLISH FILLE"
Dimitri From Paris

"MAMBO"
Flavia Lazzarini

"HELP TOO"
Little Boots

"PROPAGANDA"
Kill J

"LIGHTS"
SOHN

TALKING
STATUES

M ockery and scathing irony are typical of the Roman personality, and talking statues have for centuries offered the people a voice. Six statues make up the Congregation of Wits; located on the main streets, they bear the name of the neighborhood or the public figure they resemble. Since the fifteenth century they have literally been the voice of the people and of their malcontent. At night, the Romans would post anonymous, often irreverent and satirical messages on the statues, at first criticizing the pope and, later, the city's political figures and other authorities. It was a way for them to express their disapproval of injustice and corruption. Today the custom lives on.

Abbot Luigi

It is believed that the nickname of this statue is due to the figure's resemblance to the sexton of the nearby church of Santissimo Sudario. Set on a pedestal, this full-figured sculpture from the Late Roman period represents a magistrate wearing a toga. It was found in the area where it is still located today, close to the church of Sant'Andrea della Valle, in Piazza Vidoni, where the Theater of Pompey once stood. Weather and vandalism have taken their toll, and the statue has been restored and its head replaced on several occasions; the first time was when it was transferred to the sumptuous Palazzo Caffarelli. "I've lost my head!" was Abbot Luigi's comment at the time. It wouldn't be the last time Abbot Luigi lost his head; it happened again as recently as 2013.

EATING TIP
ROSCIOLI
via dei Giubbonari 21
+39 06 687 52 87
salumeriaroscioli.com
open 12:30-4 p.m.
and 7 p.m.-midnight
closed Sun

🚶 4 MINUTES

piazza Vidoni

THE BABOON

One of the most elegant and famous streets in the capital, Via del Babuino means "Baboon Street," named after one of Rome's ugliest statues. Reclining on one side, the statue represents a satyr, which has been made even more grotesque with the passing of time. It decorates a simple fountain that in the past was used as a water trough for horses. Proof of the statue's talkativeness is the wall behind it, which until 1990 was completely covered with graffiti.

**EATING TIP
'GUSTO AL 28**
piazza Augusto
Imperatore 28
+39 06 681 34 221
gusto.it
open 8 a.m.-midnight

 5 MINUTES

via del Babuino opposite no. 65

Il Facchino

So beautiful was this statue that the eighteenth-century architect Luigi Vanvitelli attributed it to Michelangelo, although it is in fact the work of the Florentine artist Jacopo del Conte. Commissioned by the Corporazione degli Acquaioli (Corporation of Water-Sellers) the fountain is made entirely of travertine and represents the humble door-to-door water seller (*facchino*) common before the ancient aqueducts were restored. It is the smallest of the Congregation of Wits, and also the "youngest," dating to the end of sixteenth century.

EATING TIP
BOTTEGA ROCCHI
via del Caravita 9
+39 06 678 61 91
open 9 a.m.-8 p.m.

🚶 3 MINUTES

via Lata almost at intersection with via del Corso

MADAMA LUCREZIA

This is the only female figure in the group of talking statues, and since the sixteenth century it has stood at the corner between Piazza Venezia and Piazza San Marco. The large marble bust measures almost ten feet tall and wears a shawl around its shoulders. In 1799, during the uprisings of the Roman Republic, the rebels threw the statue to the ground, breaking it into eight pieces. The next day a sign was hung from Madama Lucrezia's shoulders that read: "I can't stand it anymore!" The reference was to the bad government.

EATING TIP
TAVERNA
DEGLI AMICI
piazza Margana 37
+39 06 699 20 637
latavernadegliamici.net
open noon-11 p.m.
closed Mon

🚶 3 MINUTES

piazza San Marco

Marforio

Marforio is a marble statue from the Roman period that represents a river god. It is the second most famous talking statue, after Pasquino, and is considered to be his "partner." Often the two statues talked to each other: Pasquino asked and Marforio answered. From its original location at the Foro di Marte, opposite the Carcere Mamertino (the Mamertine Prison, in the Roman Forum), Pope Sixtus V had the statue moved to Piazza San Marco first and then the Campidoglio later. This is where it is currently located, in the courtyard of the Capitoline Museums.

EATING TIP
TERRAZZA
CAFFARELLI
Campidoglio, piazzale
Caffarelli 4
+39 06 322 04 04
terrazzacaffarelli.com
open 9:30 a.m.-7 p.m.

⚲ 2 MINUTES

Campidoglio, Cortile dei Musei Capitolini

PASQUINO

This is unquestionably the most famous talking statue, the one that led to the invention of the word *pasquinade*, meaning any type of satirical writing. Among the Congregation of Wits, it is also the one that continues to "talk" today. This marble statue, set on a pedestal, is so ruined today that anyone looking at it will find it hard to understand whom it represents (originally probably Menelaus supporting the body of Patrocles). One of the most famous pasquinades was addressed to Pope Urban VIII (born Maffeo Barberini), who had the ancient bronzes of the Pantheon's pronaos removed and fused to build the baldachin of Saint Peter's. On that occasion Pasquino exclaimed: "*Quod non fecerunt barbari, fecerunt Barberini*" (What the barbarians didn't do, Barberini did).

EATING TIP
CUL DE SAC
piazza di Pasquino 73
+39 06 688 01 094
enotecaculdesacroma.it
open noon-12:30 a.m.

🏃 2 MINUTES

piazza di Pasquino

. Playlist .

"I LOVE YOU"
Flavia Lazzarini

"NO. 1 LENT ET DOULOUREUX"
Isan

"THE MELODY"
Francesco Tristano

"CASTA DIVA"
Maria Callas

"THICK EAR"
Bent

"LOVE"
Air

"ENCORE"
Nicolas Jaar

SACRED LOVE, PROFANE LOVE

The Eternal City has always exerted a strong attraction for everyone, and many women, both the saintly and the less so, have come here driven by the wish to study, to discover their deepest spiritual side, to find or to put to the test their artistic vocation, or even to make their fortune under the protective wing of the papacy. Hosts of artistic circles, patrons, keen collectors, the emblematic gurus of moral teachings and faith, but also the avid seekers of power and wealth—all these women have had to come to terms with the Roman Catholic Church, which, for better or for worse, has consigned them to history. We have chosen the seven most emblematic of them all.

Blessed Ludovica Albertoni

If you wish to witness with your own eyes the profound faith that distinguished this Roman noblewoman, you should visit the place where she was buried, in the Altieri Chapel, near the church of San Francesco a Ripa. Born in 1474 into an aristocratic Roman family, Ludovica was forced by her parents to marry the nobleman Giacomo Della Cetera, with whom she had three daughters. After her husband passed away, Ludovica entered the Third Order of Saint Francis and devoted her life to prayer, meditation, and works of mercy. Against her family's will, she sold all her worldly possessions so that she could help the poor and the sick. She died in 1533. Gian Lorenzo Bernini portrayed her at the moment of her ecstasy in the statue placed on her funerary monument, located in the Paluzzi-Albertoni Chapel of San Francesco a Ripa church. In this magnificent composition of 1671, considered one of the finest examples of Baroque sculpture, Bernini cleverly toyed with light, material, and painting, creating a surprisingly narrative effect to portray the gentility of mystical ecstasy.

San Francesco a Ripa
piazza di San Francesco d'Assisi 88
+ 39 06 581 90 20
open 7:30 a.m.-1 p.m. and 2-7:30 p.m.
sanfrancescoaripa.com

EATING TIP
HOSTARIA LUCE
via della Luce 44
+39 06 581 48 39
hostarialuce.it
open 11 a.m.-3 p.m.
and 7-10:30 p.m.
Sun 11 a.m.-3 p.m.

 2 MINUTES

CHRISTINA, QUEEN OF SWEDEN

For those who wish to learn about the life of this intelligent, restless figure, a good place to start is a visit to the two palaces in which she stayed, Palazzo Farnese and Palazzo Corsini, and the site where she is buried in Saint Peter. Born in 1626, Christina became queen-elect at six years of age, and by 1650 her power was complete. Soon afterward, she converted to Catholicism, abdicating in favor of her cousin Charles Gustav and settling in Rome, at first in the Palazzo Farnese and later in the Palazzo Riario (now Palazzo Corsini). An anti-conformist, masculine in her ways, and gifted with great culture and intelligence, she brought together artists, musicians, and literati in her Accademia dell'Arcadia. Always the focus of lavish events and a series of rumors, Christina also mingled with people of ill repute, much to the dismay of the church that had at one time invited her to sit at the pope's table. She died in 1689 and is buried in the Vatican Grottoes of Saint Peter's, a privilege given to the Saxon kings who converted to Christianity.

Palazzo Farnese, piazza Farnese 67
Reservations at inventerrome.com
Palazzo Corsini, via della Lungara 10
San Pietro, piazza San Pietro, Città del Vaticano

CHRISTINA OF SWEDEN'S PASSIONATE LIFE SPAWNED MANY RUMORS; ONE OF THEM CONCERNED HER FRIENDSHIP WITH CARDINAL DECIO AZZOLINO, AND ANOTHER THE MURDER OF HER MASTER OF THE HORSE, MARQUESS MONALDESCHI, FOR PLOTTING AGAINST HER.

EATING TIP
PIERLUIGI
piazza de' Ricci 144
+39 06 686 87 17
pierluigi.it
open 12:30-3 p.m.
and 7:30-11:30 p.m.

🚶 4 - 16 MINUTES

Olimpia Pamphilj

It is well worth taking a walk as far as the Piazza Navona to get to know a woman who was famous neither for her beauty nor for her kindness—one who was in fact nicknamed "la Pimpaccia" because of her many wrongdoings. Born in Viterbo in 1594 into a humble family, Olimpia was destined to become a nun, but instead ended up marrying a wealthy member of the bourgeoisie who died three years later. For her second marriage, Olimpia wed Pamphilio Pamphilj, a man 27 years her senior—and penniless to boot—but whose brother would become Pope Innocent X. Her ruthless, endless effort to gain wealth, and the favoritism she showed for her brother-in-law the pope aroused loathing among the people. It was Olimpia who stole the relic of Saint Francesca Romana, later found in the abbey of San Martino al Cimino, which she owned. But she does deserve credit for one thing: she convinced Pope Innocent X to choose, among the many artists suggested, Gian Lorenzo Bernini to decorate the Piazza Navona. Indeed, it is thanks to her that we can now enjoy the immense beauty of the Fountain of the Four Rivers.

Palazzo Pamphilj Via del Corso 305
+39 06 679 73 23
open 9 a.m.-7 p.m.
doriapamphilj.it/roma

TWO YEARS EARLIER, WHEN INNOCENT X DIED, SHE'D PULLED TWO CRATES FILLED WITH GOLD FROM UNDER HIS BED AND TOOK THEM AWAY. TO THOSE WHO ASKED THAT SHE CONTRIBUTE TO THE EXPENSES FOR HER BROTHER-IN-LAW'S FUNERAL, SHE ANSWERED: "WHAT CAN A POOR WIDOW POSSIBLY DO TO HELP?"

EATING TIP
SETTIMIO
AL PELLEGRINO
via del Pellegrino 117
+39 06 688 01 978
open noon-3:30 p.m.
and 7 p.m.-midnight
closed Sun

 7 MINUTES

Saint Catherine of Siena

Saint Catherine was proclaimed the patron saint of Italy in 1939 by Pope Pius XII, along with Saint Francis of Assisi, and co-patron saint of Europe by Pope John Paul II. Her body rests in the church of Santa Maria Sopra Minerva. Born in Siena in 1347, the daughter of a dyer and the youngest of twenty-five children, Caterina Benincasa was twelve years old when she refused to marry the man who had been chosen for her, instead embracing religious life and entering a convent. She spent much of her life helping the sick and wrote about 380 letters championing church reform. Little is left of her home in today's Piazza Santa Chiara, where she settled in 1378; one of the rooms is now a chapel, and all that remains of the original architecture are the ceiling beams.

THE ELEPHANT SUPPORTING THE OBELISK IN THE PIAZZA IS NICKNAMED "*IL PULCIN DELLA MINERVA*" (MINERVA'S CHICK). LEGEND HAS IT THAT BERNINI WAS FORCED BY THE POPE, WHO WAS (UNFOUNDEDLY) CONCERNED ABOUT THE MONUMENT'S STABILITY, TO ADD A STONE CUBE UNDER THE ANIMAL'S BELLY. SINCE DOING SO MADE THE SCULPTURE LOOK MUCH HEAVIER, PEOPLE BEGAN TO CALL IT "*IL PORCINO*" (THE PIG), WHICH THEN BECAME "*PURCINO*," ROMAN DIALECT FOR *PULCINO*, OR "CHICK."

Santa Maria Sopra Minerva
piazza della Minerva 42
+ 39 06 699 20 384
open 7:30 a.m.-7 p.m.
Sat 7:30 a.m.-noon and 3:30-7 p.m.
Sun 8 a.m.-12:30 p.m. and 3:30-7 p.m.
santamariasopraminerva.it

EATING TIP
TRATTORIA DER PALLARO
largo di Pallaro 15
+39 06 688 01 488
trattoriaderpallaro.com
open 12:30-3 p.m.
and 7-11 p.m.

 7 MINUTES

Saint Cecilia

The church of Santa Cecilia in Trastevere stands on what was once the home of Saint Cecilia, a Roman noblewoman who lived between the second and third centuries, converted to Christianity, and was a benefactress of the popes. The saint is also the patron saint of musicians because, according to tradition, during her wedding to the nobleman Valerian, while the music was being played, "Cecilia sang in her heart to the Lord." And indeed the Accademia di Santa Cecilia is named after her, the city's most prestigious music academy and one of the most important in the world. Cecilia also convinced her husband to convert, but the two spouses were tortured and killed for their faith. The story goes that Cecilia sang her praise to the Lord while being martyred. When the church of Santa Cecilia in Trastevere was refurbished for the Jubilee of 1600, the sarcophagus of her remains was unearthed and the martyr was found to be miraculously preserved. Pietro Cavallini's masterpiece, the mosaic cycle dedicated to the *Life of the Virgin Mary*, is preserved in the church.

Santa Cecilia piazza di Santa Cecilia 22
+ 39 06 454 92 739
open 10 a.m.-12:30 p.m. and 4-6 p.m.
Sun 11:30 a.m.-12:30 p.m. and 4-6 p.m.

EATING TIP
AI MARMI
viale di Trastevere 53
+39 06 580 09 19
open 7 p.m.-2 a.m.
closed Wed

 5 MINUTES

SAINT PRASSEDE AND SAINT PUDENZIANA

Named after the two sisters, the churches of Santa Pudenziana and Santa Prassede rise up on the Esquiline Hill, just a few hundred yards from each other. The story goes that the two young women were the daughters of a Roman senator named Pudens, who allowed the Apostle Peter to lodge with him. The two women, devoted to prayer, had a baptistery built, where they converted and baptized many pagans. Both of them were persecuted and killed. Prassede was only sixteen years old when she died, while Pudenziana, before dying, managed to have two churches built, which were later turned into basilicas. The Basilica of Santa Prassede is especially famous for being one of the major examples of Byzantine art in Rome, thanks to a cycle of stunning ninth-century mosaics covering the apse, the choir, and the Chapel of San Zenone—depicting the apostle Peter and Paul, the Transfiguration, the Virgin, Saint Prassede, Saint Pudenziana and Saint Agnes.

Santa Prassede via di Santa Prassede 9
+ 39 06 488 24 56
open 7 a.m.-12 p.m. and 3-6:30 p.m.
Santa Pudenziana via Urbana 160
+39 06 481 46 22
open 8:30 a.m.-noon and 3-6 p.m.

AT THE BACK OF THE LEFT NAVE, IN THE CHURCH OF SANTA PRASSEDE, IS AN EIGHTEENTH-CENTURY AEDICULE (SMALL SHRINE) WITH A BLACK MARBLE SLAB. LEGEND HAS IT THAT THIS WAS THE STONE PRASSEDE USED TO SLEEP ON, AS WELL AS THE ONE USED TO SEAL HER GRAVE.

EATING TIP
ENOTECA CAVOUR
via Cavour 313
+39 06 678 54 96
cavour313.it
open 12:30-2:45 p.m.
and 7:30 p.m.-12:30 a.m.

🚶 9 - 11 MINUTES

SAINT TERESA OF ÁVILA

Teresa Sánchez de Cepeda Dávila y Ahumada was born in 1515 into a noble and religious Spanish family from the province of Ávila. At the age of twenty she entered a convent, and after a difficult spiritual journey she became one of the leading figures of Catholic reform. The reformer of Carmel and mother of the Discalced Carmelites, Teresa founded several monasteries and wrote many texts presenting the doctrine. She died in ecstasy in Alba de Tormes on October 4, 1582, and was proclaimed blessed in 1610 and a saint in 1622. In the mid-seventeenth century, Gian Lorenzo Bernini dedicated the *Ecstasy of Saint Theresa*, one of his most spectacular works, to her. This marble and bronze sculpture can be viewed in the Cornaro Chapel of the church of Santa Maria della Vittoria. The interior of the chapel is as if transformed into a theater, and the figures in the group are framed by rays of light filtering down from above, illuminating the scene. Visitors feel as though they are witnessing the saint's ecstasy.

OBSERVE TO EITHER SIDE OF THE ALTAR THE TWO BOXES REPRESENTING THE MEMBERS OF THE CORNARO FAMILY: THEY SEEM TO BE WATCHING THE SAINT'S ECSTASY WITH THE DETACHMENT OF TWO SPECTATORS, EXCHANGING COMMENTS, THE WAY PEOPLE DO AT THEATER.

Santa Maria della Vittoria
via XX Settembre 17
+39 06 427 40 571
open 7 a.m.-12 p.m. and 3:30-7 p.m.
chiesasantamariavittoriaroma.it

EATING TIP
IL GIRASOLE
via del Boschetto 28
+39 06 456 15 227
trattoriamontiilgirasole.it
open 12-3 p.m.
and 6:30-11:30 p.m.

 12 MINUTES

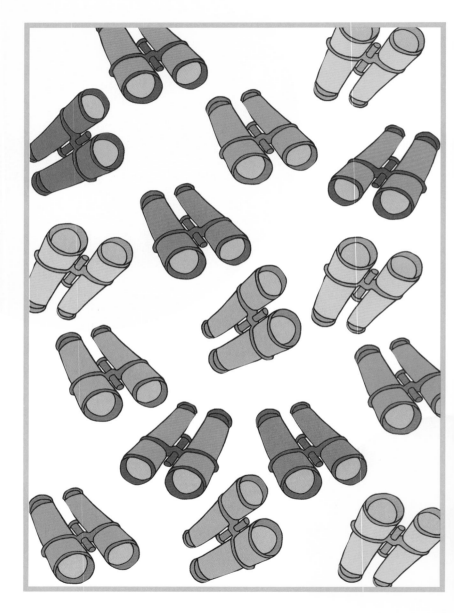

BAREFOOT IN THE PARK

- Parks and Villas
- The Botanical Gardens
- The Orange Garden
- Villa Ada

- Villa Borghese
- Villa Doria Pamphilj
- Villa Sciarra
- Villa Torlonia

. Playlist .

"LATELY"
Massive Attack

"GONE BABY, DON'T BE LONG"
Erykah Badu

"PAWN SHOP CLOSE"
Populous

"EVERYDAY PEOPLE"
Arrested Development

"EXPERIENCE 5" (FLAVIA LAZZARINI RMX)
Davide Orkestar

"TEN MINUTES"
Tensnake

"CLOSURE"
Jill Scott

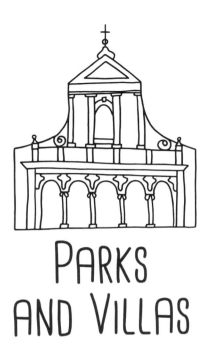

PARKS
AND VILLAS

I n the fifteenth century, the frequent flooding of the Tiber River and poor management of the sewer system encouraged noble families to move to their villas in the country, just outside the city, during summertime. The country was historically the place for *otium* (idleness) and the pleasures of the soul, and it was often the heart of cultural life, as opposed to the *negotium* (business)—the frenetic activity linked to public life—and the life of vice in the city. Either built from scratch or the result of excellent refurbishment, with their beautiful parks and magnificent architecture, these seven villas offer a charming portrait revealing the customs of the most powerful aristocratic families during that period.

THE BOTANICAL GARDENS

Founded in the fourteenth century as "gardens of the simple," used to cultivate medicinal herbs (also known as simple or officinal), the land was later turned into an orchard and kitchen garden for the papal court. In the sixteenth century it officially became Rome's botanical gardens under the direction of the prefect Michele Mercati, the pope's physician. Nearly thirty acres of land are filled with over 3,000 plant species, including aromatic and aquatic plants, centuries-old trees, rose gardens, and evergreens. There is a lovely Japanese garden and a garden of fragrances that will make this visit memorable even for the visually impaired. The eighteenth-century grand staircase is the work of the architect Ferdinando Fuga. Today the botanical gardens are the seat of the La Sapienza University of Rome's Department of Environmental Biology, where research is carried out in the fields of botany, ecology, and the natural sciences. Exhibitions and lectures are periodically held here.

entrance: largo Cristina di Svezia 24
+ 39 06 499 17 107
open Mar-Oct 9 a.m.-6:30 p.m. closed Sun;
Nov-Feb 9 a.m.-5:30 p.m. closed Sun;
ortobotanicoitalia.it

THE TWO MONUMENTAL PLANE TREES AT THE ENTRANCE DATE TO THE SEVENTEENTH CENTURY, AND THE ROSE GARDEN CONTAINS ABOUT SIXTY DIFFERENT VARIETIES. BUT THAT'S NOT ALL: THE GREENHOUSE COLLECTS SOME 400 SPECIES OF ORCHIDS!

PICNIC TIP
LA PROSCIUTTERIA
TRASTEVERE
via della Scala 71
+39 06 645 62 839
laprosciutteria.com
open 11 a.m.-11:30 p.m.

 5 MINUTES

THE ORANGE GARDEN

Parco Savello is more commonly known as the Orange Garden for the large number of Seville or bitter orange trees that grow there. It once surrounded an ancient fortress built in the late thirteenth century over what was left of the Crescenzi Castle, which dated from three centuries earlier. The embankment overlooking the Tiber offers one of the most breathtaking views of Rome. Today's symmetrical layout was designed in 1932 by the architect Raffaele De Vico. The main entrance features a curious fountain comprising a thermal bath in Egyptian granite and a mascaron with frowning eyebrows and thick moustache sculpted by Bartolomeo Bassi according to a design by Giacomo Della Porta.

IF YOU WALK DOWN THE ANCIENT ROMAN ROAD KNOWN AS THE CLIVO DI ROCCA SAVELLA, YOU WILL COME TO PIAZZA DELLA BOCCA DELLA VERITÀ (MOUTH OF TRUTH). THE TIME HAS COME TO PUT YOURSELF TO THE TEST. PLACE YOUR HAND INSIDE THE MARBLE MASCARON AND SAY SOMETHING. LEGEND HAS IT THAT IF YOU LIE, YOUR HAND WILL GET A BITE!

entrance: piazza Pietro d'Illiria, via di S. Sabina and clivo di Rocca Savella
Oct-Feb 7 a.m.-6 p.m.;
Mar and Sep 7 a.m.-8 p.m.;
Apr-Aug 7 a.m.-9 p.m.
www.sovraintendenzaroma.it

PICNIC TIP
IN CIBO VERITAS
Mercato Rionale di Testaccio, Box 57
via Beniamino Franklin
+39 338 842 46 22

 9 MINUTES

VILLA ADA

This ancient and vast farming estate was reorganized into gardens in the eighteenth century by the Princes Pallavicini and later purchased by the Savoy family as a hunting estate. The name stems from the main building, the royal villa that King Victor Emmanuel II had built, and purchased at the time of his death by the Swiss Count Tellfner, who dedicated it to his wife Ada. The villa park, in addition to the countless trees, hosts a surprising variety of plants, including a rare aquatic conifer imported from Tibet in 1940. This site is also interesting from a historical-archaeological point of view; thanks to its closeness to the Via Salaria, the oldest consular road in Rome, there are traces here of Christian sepulchers, necropolises, and catacombs. In addition to the royal villa, the park also hosts several buildings, including the Temple of Flora and the stables, and a few examples of industrial archaeology, such as the "bunker," the royal air-raid shelter with armored doors that in the 1960s still had its original furnishings. Villa Ada is now public property and hosts musical festivals and other forms of entertainment.

entrance: via Salaria, via di Ponte Salario, via di Monte Antenne, via Panama
open 7 a.m. to sunset
villaada.org

MOST OF THE TUNNELS OF THE VAST CATACOMB OF SAINT PRISCILLA, INTERWOVEN FOR MANY MILES ON TWO LEVELS, ARE LOCATED BELOW VILLA ADA. OWING TO THE LARGE NUMBER OF MARTYRS BURIED HERE, THIS CEMETERY WAS CALLED "*REGINA CATACUMBARUM.*" THE ENTRANCE IS AT VIA SALARIA 430.

PICNIC TIP
LA PIADINERIA,
SUSINA CAFFETTERIA
BISTRÒ
via Chiana 87a
+ 39 06 858 57 162
open 9 a.m.-11 p.m.
closed Sun

🚶 9 MINUTES

VILLA BORGHESE

Superb fountains, enchanting lakes, and Italian-style gardens make this villa, which was owned by the Borghese family until the twentieth century and then acquired by the state, one of the city's most precious treasures. Inside the park are so many exhibition sites that it is often referred to as "Museum Park." It includes the Galleria Borghese (formerly the noble summerhouse of Cardinal Scipione Borghese), which currently houses some of the most important Italian works from the sixteenth to the seventeenth centuries, the Museo Canonica, the Casa del Cinema in the Casina delle Rose, and the Museo Carlo Bilotti. The Villa Borghese is a source of inspiration for artists, poets, and musicians and an unforgettable experience for all who visit.

THE VILLA BORGHESE HAS ALSO BEEN CALLED THE "GREEN HEART OF ROME." LOOK AT A MAP OF THE PARK AND YOU'LL SEE WHY.

entrance: via Aldrovandi, via Raimondi (2 entrances), via Pinciana (2 entrances), piazzale San Paolo del Brasile, piazzale Flaminio, piazzale Cervantes
open: always
www.sovraintendenzaroma.it

PICNIC TIP
GINA EAT & DRINK
via di San Sebastianello 7
+39 06 678 02 51
open 11 a.m.-7 p.m.

 10 MINUTES

VILLA DORIA PAMPHILJ

Among the largest and most beautiful villas with a park in Rome was the country estate of the noble Pamphilj family. In the mid-nineteenth century, the estate, together with the bordering Villa Corsini, was turned into a farm. After changing hands several times, the villa became state property in the mid-1800s and was opened to the public in 1972. The villa is where the Italian government officially receives its guests. What makes a visit here special is the wealth of art and architecture that has been accumulated over the centuries—from the remains of a Roman aqueduct to funerary structures, from late medieval artifacts to splendid works of Baroque art and architecture commissioned by Pope Innocent X from Algardi, Bernini, and Grimaldi, not to mention the countless architectural gems that make the villa a treasure trove of works by Italy's major artists and architects.

entrance: via di San Pancrazio, via Aurelia Antica, via Leone XII, largo Martin Luther King, via Vitellia, via della Nocetta open Mar-Sep 7 a.m.-8 p.m; Oct-Feb 7 a.m.-6 p.m; Apr-Aug 7 a.m.-9 p.m. villapamphili.it

BEFORE (OR AFTER) A VISIT TO THE MAGNIFICENT PARK, YOU WILL WANT TO EXPERIENCE THE CURIOUS OPTICAL EFFECT OF VIA PICCOLOMINI. THIS STRAIGHT, PERFECTLY LEVEL PATH MEASURING ALMOST 1,000 FEET IN LENGTH OFFERS A MARVELOUS VIEW OF SAINT PETER'S DOME. STAND IN THE MIDDLE OF THE PATH AND LOOK CAREFULLY. IF YOU WALK BACKWARD, THE DOME GETS BIGGER; IF YOU WALK FORWARD, IT GETS SMALLER!

PICNIC TIP
VIVIBISTROT
Villa Doria Pamphilj,
entrance on via Vitellia 102
+39 06 582 75 40
vivibistrot.com

 2 MINUTES

Villa Sciarra

The villa, named after one of its owners, Prince Maffeo Sciarra, in ancient times was known as the sacred wood of the nymph Furrina, and it truly is a landscape masterpiece thanks to the presence of over 100 plant species of fruits and flowers, both exotic and Mediterranean. When the magnolias bloom in spring, the Villa Sciarra resembles something out of a fairy tale. Legend has it that Cleopatra stayed at the villa when Caesar's Garden was here. If you enter from Via Dandolo, you'll see the lovely Wurts aviary where white peacocks were once bred (the villa was at one time called the Villa of the White Peacocks). Directly opposite is the lovely fountain of Satyrs from a Lombard palace owned by the Visconti. The park is filled with countless eighteenth-century statues and fountains, including the exquisite fountain of the Putti and of the Tartaruga, as well as the Junonic statue of Astrology.

entrance: viale delle Mura Gianicolensi 11
+ 39 06 06 06
open Mar-Sep 7am-8pm;
Oct-Feb 7 a.m.-6 p.m;
Apr-Aug 7 a.m.-9 p.m.
www.sovraintendenzaroma.it

THE VILLA WAS PURCHASED BY GEORGE AND HENRIETTA WURTS, HEIRS TO TWO OF THE RICHEST FAMILIES IN PHILADELPHIA AND IMPASSIONED COLLECTORS WHO LIVED IN MADRID, FLORENCE, SAINT PETERSBURG, AND, FROM 1893, ROME. AFTER GEORGE'S DEATH, HENRIETTA PAID HOMAGE TO ROME BY DONATING THE VILLA TO THE STATE ON THE CONDITION THAT IT BE USED AS A PUBLIC PARK.

PICNIC TIP
I SUPPLÌ
via San Francesco
a Ripa 137
+39 06 589 71 10
open 9:30 a.m.-10 p.m.
closed Sun

 12 MINUTES

[129]

Villa Torlonia

It started out as a farming estate owned by the Pamphilj family and was later acquired by the Torlonia family, who in the eighteenth century hired the architect Valadier to design the park, transform the existing buildings, and build the stables. Later, other artists contributed to the originality of the villa by working on the landscape and designing a surprising number of eclectic structures. The noble casino (summerhouse) hosts the Museo della Scuola Romana, with numerous paintings and sculptures by artists from the first half of twentieth century; it is connected by an elegantly decorated underground tunnel to the Casino of the Princes, where Alessandro Torlonia once held lavish events and which currently hosts the school archive. The Casina delle Civette, built in the mid-nineteenth century by Giuseppe Jappelli, is decorated with magnificent glasswork by Duilio Cambellotti. For years it was the official residence of Benito Mussolini, becoming one of the city's public parks in 1978.

entrance: via Nomentana 70,
via Siracusa, via Spallanzani
+39 06 06 08
open Apr-Sep 7.a.m.-10:30 p.m;
Oct-Mar 7 a.m.-7 p.m.
www.sovraintendenzaroma.it

When the Via Nomentana was expanded in the early twentieth century, Villa Torlonia's park was reduced and some of the buildings demolished, among them the main entrance with sphinxes (two of which are now in the Casino of the Princes), a large amphitheater, and the Chapel of Saint Alexander.

PICNIC TIP
LIBRERIA KAPPA BISTROT
viale Ipocrate 113/117
+39 06 454 75 580
libreriakappabistrot.com
open 8 a.m.-12:30 a.m.
closed Sun

 12 MINUTES

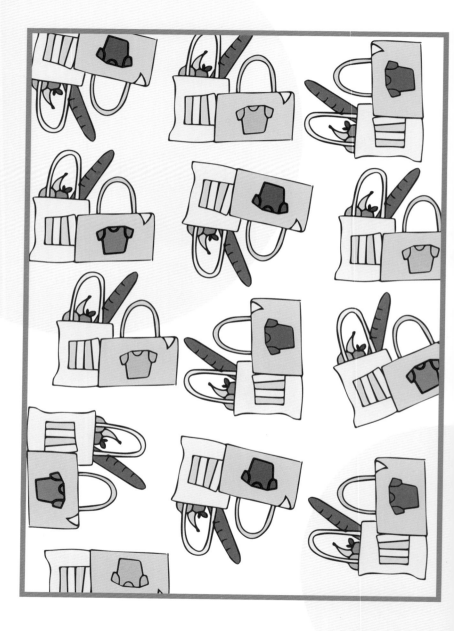

SHOPPING

- Discovering the Markets
- The Borghetto Flaminio Market
- The Campo de' Fiori Market
- The Monti Market
- Piazza delle Coppelle Market
- Piazza Monte d'Oro Market
- Porta Portese Market
- Via Sannio Market

DISCOVERING THE MARKETS

There's always something new to see while strolling around the multicolored market stands, a genuine popular tradition of the Eternal City that is part and parcel with its culture. The wide variety of historical as well as trendy neighborhood markets offers many opportunities to find exactly what you've always wanted. Let yourself be enchanted by the lively, colorful Roman feel of these seven markets, with their visitors, sellers, and curiosity seekers. And never settle for the first price! Be sure to bargain . . . This, too, is part of the experience.

THE BORGHETTO FLAMINIO MARKET

This is the Italian capital's chicest vintage market. Since 1994 it has been set up inside a former body shop, and while walking from stand to stand you'll probably meet actors, filmmakers, musicians, and artists in search of some antique, vintage clothing and handbags or trunks from way back when. It's easy to find entire collections of 1950s American costume jewelry in this market. So even if you're not looking for anything in particular, you're bound to find something to buy.

THE FRENCH CALL IT A VIDE-GRENIER (ATTIC-EMPTYING), AND IT'S DONE WHEN YOU'RE PLANNING TO MOVE OR NEED TO MAKE ROOM IN YOUR HOUSE. NONPROFESSIONAL SELLERS DISPLAYING USED OBJECTS, LOW PRICES, AND INFORMAL DEALINGS ARE CHARACTERISTIC OF THESE MARKETS, WHICH ARE POPULAR IN ENGLISH-SPEAKING COUNTRIES, TOO.

EATING TIP
TREEBAR
via Flaminia 226
+39 06 326 52 754
treebar.it
Tue-Sun 12:30-3:30 p.m.
and 6:30 p.m.-1:30 a.m.
Mon 6:30 p.m.-1:30 a.m.

 9 MINUTES

piazza della Marina 22
open Sun 10 a.m.-7 p.m.

THE CAMPO DE' FIORI MARKET

This is no doubt Rome's most famous food market, as well as one of its oldest. Under the stern and imposing gaze of the statue of Giordano Bruno, which stands at the center of the square, is an intricate labyrinth of stalls that will completely surround you with the fragrance of its spices and "zero-kilometer" specialties that the vendors will convince you to taste. Countless regulars visit the market each day in search of the freshest produce and in-season fruit and vegetables. The flower stalls are the finest in the city and contribute to making the square one of the most pleasant places to be in the morning.

AS YOU WALK DOWN VIA DEL PELLEGRINO DON'T BE TOO SCARED TO CROSS THE DARK AND NARROW ARCH OF THE ACETARI, WHICH GETS ITS NAME FROM THE PEOPLE WHO SOLD THE WATER THAT CAME FROM THE EPONYMOUS ROMAN FOUNTAIN. THIS WATER, WHICH WAS SAID TO TASTE LIKE VINEGAR, WAS AT ONE TIME BELIEVED TO DO A WORLD OF GOOD FOR THE KIDNEYS AND THE OTHER ORGANS. THE INNER COURTYARD IS A CORNER STRAIGHT OUT OF THE MIDDLE AGES!

EATING TIP
FORNO CAMPO DE' FIORI
Campo de' Fiori 22
vicolo del Gallo 14
+39 06 688 06 662
fornocampodefiori.com
open 7:30 a.m.-2:30 p.m.
& 4:45-8 p.m. closed Sun

🚶 2 MINUTES

Campo de' Fiori
open 6 a.m.-2 p.m.
closed Sun

The Monti Market

In the heart of the city's trendiest neighborhood, the Monti quarter, this eponymous market is a workshop for emerging artisans on the Roman scene. But it's not just that. Visitors also have the chance to discover young talents displaying their wares on colorful stands. Vintage clothes and costume jewelry, curios, designer fashions by unknowns, and lots more—you'll find a vast assortment of objects in this big little market set up in the conference room of the Grand Hotel Palatino that's always accompanied by a cheerful DJ set. Popular with neighborhood residents, this urban market is one of the city's liveliest.

THE RISE OF THE BORGIA DYNASTY IS LINKED TO A LEGEND FROM ANCIENT ROME: IN THIS VERY PLACE, AT ONE TIME CALLED VICUS SCELERATUS, SERVIUS TULLIUS, THE SIXTH KING OF ROME, WAS MURDERED BY THE HAND OF HIS DAUGHTER TULLIA MINOR AND HER HUSBAND, LUCIUS TARQUINIUS THE SUPERB. TULLIA DROVE HER CARRIAGE OVER HER FATHER'S BODY, INJURING AND ULTIMATELY KILLING HIM.

EATING TIP
ZIA ROSETTA
Via Urbana 54
+39 06 310 52 516
ziarosetta.com
open 11 a.m.-10 p.m.
closed Mon

 1 MINUTE

via Leonina 46
open Sep-Jun
Sat and Sun 10 a.m.-8 p.m.

PIAZZA DELLE COPPELLE MARKET

Beyond the Pantheon, in the delightful Piazza delle Coppelle, you'll find this small but intriguing neighborhood market, where you can buy the best of the season's produce, rich selections of cheese and cured meats from outside the city, and fruits and flowers. Bright colors and a warm atmosphere right in the heart of historical Rome.

EATING TIP
PIZZERIA
IL LEONCINO
via del Leoncino 28
+39 06 686 77 57
open 1-3 p.m.
and 7 p.m.-midnight;
Sun 7 p.m.-midnight
closed Wed

🏃 6 MINUTES

piazza delle Coppelle
open 6 a.m.-2 p.m.
closed Sun

Piazza Monte d'Oro Market

This is perhaps the smallest of the city's neighborhood markets, but inside you'll find everything a respectable market should have. The fruit and vegetable stand is a triumph of aromas and colors, as is the delicatessen, which is surrounded all day long by people buying *pizza bianca* that can't get any better than this. You'll be surprised to find this old market right in the middle of the city's fashion quarter, and very close to via del Corso.

largo Monte d'Oro
open 6 a.m.-2 p.m.
closed Sun

EATING TIP
SETTIMIO ALL'ARANCIO
via dell'Arancio 50
+39 06 687 61 19
settimioallarancio.it
open noon-4 p.m.
and 7 p.m.-midnight
closed Sun

 2 MINUTES

PORTA PORTESE MARKET

This is Rome's historic market par excellence, a must for collectors everywhere. On Sundays from 6 a.m. to 2 p.m., antiques, mid-century modern furnishings, books, records, vintage clothing, heirlooms, and objects of all kinds can be found here, encouraging you to browse from stand to stand and peruse the often unusual objects for sale.

THE PORTA PORTESE, FOR WHICH THE MARKET IS NAMED, IS NOT THE ORIGINAL PORTA PORTUENSIS FROM THE ROMAN PERIOD. POPE URBAN VIII HAD IT BUILT IN THE SEVENTEENTH CENTURY.

EATING TIP
LO SCOPETTARO
lungotevere Testaccio 7
+39 06 574 24 08
loscopettaroroma.com
open 12:30-2:30 p.m.
and 7:30-10:30 p.m.

 4 MINUTES

entrance: from piazza Ippolito Nievo, on viale Trastevere, or from Porta Portese, on piazza di Porta Portese
open Sun 6 a.m.-2 p.m.

Via Sannio Market

This is the place for vintage clothing enthusiasts. The first stands you'll see sell objects and military garments, from camouflage gear to parkas to army boots. Continuing along you'll discover many other stands offering clothing, accessories, and footwear, as well as secondhand and theater costumes, hats, glittering eveningwear, affordable cashmere items, and retro eyeglasses.

via Sannio
open 7:30 a.m.-2 p.m.
closed Sun

EATING TIP
HOSTARIA CANNAVOTA
piazza di San Giovanni
in Laterano 20
+39 06 772 05 007
cannavota.it
open 12:45-3 p.m.
and 7:45-11 p.m.

 9 MINUTES

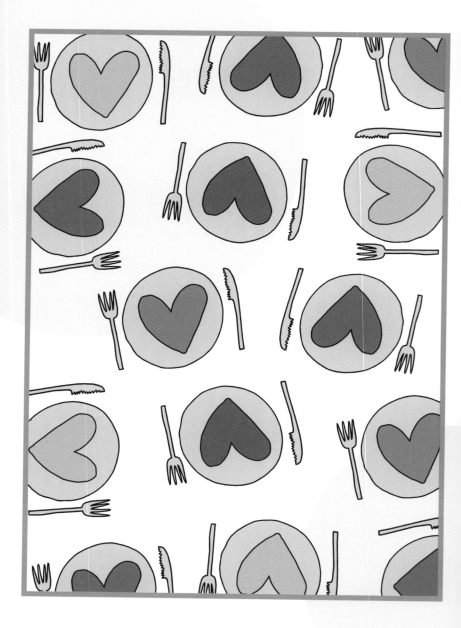

A Taste
of Rome

Ai Marmi

In this pizzeria located in the popular Trastevere neighborhood the pizza and supplì (rice croquettes) are to die for, and all the other fried specialties are delicious . . . so delicious it's hard not to overdo it. The place is roomy, noisy, crowded, and fun. The tables outdoors seem to be taking up more and more space, and it's always a treat to eat while watching the comings and goings in the heart of Trastevere. A fun fact: humorously referred to by the Romans as "the morgue" because of the marble-topped counters and tables, it seems the restaurant got its nickname from director Pier Paolo Pasolini.

viale di Trastevere 53
+39 06 580 09 19
open 7 p.m.-2 a.m.
closed Wed

Antico Cafè Ruschena

Breakfast here is a pleasant, relaxing experience, whether in the large rooms inside or outdoors, under the great arches of Palazzo Blumenstihl and overlooking the Tiber River. This is one of the capital's historic cafés, popular with the Romans, who consider it an elegant place for the first meal of the day. This is where you'll get the best croissants in Rome and some of the finest pastries, such as cassate (sponge cake filled with ricotta), cannoli, and almond paste cookies. For a taste of Sicily, try a croissant with coffee granita (flavored crushed ice).

lungotevere dei Mellini 1
+39 06 321 10 016
open 6:30 a.m.-9 p.m.
anticocaferuschena.it

Assunta Madre

Bar Rosati

Behind Campo de' Fiori, in the poetic Via Giulia, you'll be charmed by the flavors and aromas of this special seafood restaurant, famous for the freshness of its ingredients. Excellent raw fish and a rich antipasto of cooked fish are a prelude to a series of exquisite delicacies, including the Catalan astice (small lobster) they're famous for, with a perfect balance of ingredients.

Famous for the superior quality of its chocolates and pastries, not to mention the elegance of the Art Déco decor, Bar Rosati is the right place to go for breakfast or a drink, sitting at one of the tables in the sumptuous setting of Piazza del Popolo. In the 1960s and '70s, this was the haunt of artists and intellectuals, including Mario Schifano, Tano Festa, Franco Angeli, Giosetta Fioroni, Mario Ceroli, Renato Mambor, Jannis Kounellis, Pino Pascali, Alberto Moravia, Pier Paolo Pasolini, Renato Guttuso, Ennio Flaiano. Thanks to the excellent service, this pause in the day will feel very chic.

via Giulia 14
+39 06 688 06 972
open 7 p.m.-midnight
assuntamadre.com

piazza del Popolo 5
+39 06 322 58 59
open 7:30 a.m.-11 p.m.
barrosati.com

LA BOTTEGA DEL CAFFÈ

LA BUVETTE

Evergreen climbing plants shelter the outdoor tables, which are kept warm in winter, too, and offer an intimate, enchanting corner for breakfast. Take in the lovely view overlooking the Catecumeni Fountain and the square that, from the earliest hours of the day, is filled with tourists and neighborhood residents. The sweet and savory pastry is simple, yet special.

This historical cafeteria located at the Tridente (the three straight roads that run from Piazza del Popolo southward) was inspired by old French railway stations. It is a trendy location for those wishing to relax in an elegant Northern European atmosphere and enjoy a meal served with the same elegance and courtesy. From the small but fancy tables outside one can watch the to-ing and fro-ing of passersby from Via del Corso to Via del Babuino.

piazza della Madonna
dei Monti 5
+39 06 474 15 78
open 8 a.m.-2 a.m.

via Vittoria 44
+39 06 679 03 83
open 7:30 a.m.-11 p.m.
Sun 8:30 a.m.-3 p.m.

Caffè Novecento

This cozy bohemian venue, decorated with turn-of-the-century objects and French bistro tables, is popular for its homemade cakes, pastries, and muffins. The delicate, discreet service and old-fashioned atmosphere are ideal for a pause to relax and think. Patrons can also choose to work here quietly while munching on a savory pie or sipping a smoothie, surrounded by the evocative early twentieth-century atmosphere.

Caffè Propaganda

A design concept that's a nod to the French, with crystal chandeliers, antique silver trays, and walls clad in the white tilework typical of Paris Métro stations, has turned this café into a lounge for the Roman and international jet set. The menu is a scrumptious mix of tradition and innovation, and the ingredients are always top quality. One of the owners is the DJ and producer Giancarlo Battafarano, founder of the Goa Club of Rome, so you're guaranteed good background music, too. It's worth a visit just for the drinks, skillfully mixed, to be sipped at the counter.

via del Governo Vecchio 12
+39 06 686 52 42
open 9 a.m.-10 p.m.

via Claudia 15
+39 06 945 34 255
open noon-2 a.m.
closed Mon
caffepropaganda.it

Cul de Sac

Dal Bolognese

Located behind Piazza Navona, this restaurant-bistro was a pioneer of Roman wine bars because of its cellar, which boasts 1,500 labels and only the finest charcuterie and cheeses. Though the look is definitely French, the Cul de Sac is genuinely Roman. In fact, it serves beef tail stew, lasagna, and involtini (stuffed rolled meat), besides dishes inspired by Northern European cuisine, like onion soup, topik, and baba ghanoush.

An aristocratic setting, an exclusive view, and elegant atmosphere: a truly extraordinary location for one of Rome's finest restaurants overlooking Piazza del Popolo, whose clientele is the crème de la crème. Emilian specialties are served here—classical, delicious, and genuine. Tortellini soup is the most popular dish and a must, even when it's hot outside. Reservations are required; dress code: formal dark.

piazza di Pasquino 73
+39 06 688 01 094
open noon-12:30 a.m.
enotecaculdesacroma.it

piazza del Popolo 1
+39 06 322 22 799
open 12:45-3 p.m.
and 8:15-11 p.m.
dalbolognese.it

Dar Filettaro

Let your nose lead you down Via dei Giubbonari and you can't miss it: crisp batter and the irresistible flavor of fried fillet of cod, a Roman tradition, to be eaten hot (Chef Marcello Cortesi's specialty). You should also try the Roman-style puntarelle (chicory leaf ribs) tossed with anchovies and garlic, the fried zucchini, the bread and butter. And everything can be taken to-go. Don't stop here if you're on a diet—it's irresistible!

largo dei Librari 88
+39 06 686 40 18
open 5-11:40 p.m.
closed Sun

Domenico dal 1968

In the setting of an old trattoria decorated in retro style with collections of mirrors hanging on the walls, Domenico dal 1968 welcomes its clientele with simple yet surprising Roman dishes made using local farm produce. We suggest maltagliati (rough cut pasta) with baby clams and broccoli, fried calamari and shrimp, fried calf's brain and sweetbreads, and fried artichokes. A favorite here is the spaghettoni all'amatriciana (cured pork cheek, pecorino, and tomato) cooked by a native of Amatrice, the town this delicious dish was named after. The strictly local wine list changes often, offering a variety of new wines from the Lazio region.

via Satrico, 23/25
+39 06 704 94 602
open 12:30-3 p.m. and
8-11:30 p.m.; Mon 8-11:30 p.m.
closed Sun
domenicodal1968.it

Enoteca Corsi

Enoteca La Torre

This is truly a traditional Roman trattoria, with its typical rustic setting and a decidedly wooden decor. The menu is filled with Rome's favorite dishes, including excellent first and second courses, and it ends with delicious homemade dolci (desserts). Maybe because it has always been family run, the atmosphere here is warm, and you can expect the staff to be kind and pleasant.

In the prestigious Villa Laetitia, built in 1911 by Armando Brasini and owned by the Fendi family, you'll be able to savor the haute cuisine of Chef Danilo Ciavattini: genuine flavors from carefully selected ingredients that respect the changing of the seasons. The elegant offerings and careful attention to detail of the decor, overseen personally by Anna Venturini Fendi, as well as the special wine list, make eating here a complete gastronomic experience. Dress code: cocktail.

via del Gesù 87/88
+39 06 679 08 21
Mon-Sat 9 a.m.-7 p.m. Thur and Fri 9 a.m.-midnight
closed Sun
enotecacorsi.com

lungotevere delle Armi 22/23
+39 06 456 68 304
Tue-Sat 12:30-3 p.m.
and 7:30-1 p.m. Mon 7:30-11pm
closed Sun
enotecalatorreroma.com

FELICE

FIAMMETTA

The deliciousness of home cooking passed down from generation to generation, the authentic setting, and the staff's friendly manners have made this one of the city's most famous trattorie. Sitting at the tables at the heart of Testaccio quarter, you might as easily find a blue-collar worker on his lunch break as a famous TV star. You'll be intrigued by the honesty of the flavors and the typically Roman atmosphere. The specialty here is spaghetti with cacio e pepe (pecorino cheese and pepper), an absolute must!

Family run since 1944, Fiammetta serves delicious and carefully prepared traditional Roman cuisine: simple dishes, large portions, and excellent pizza. When the weather's nice, you'll want to eat outside for a pleasant break from all the hustle and bustle. Just a stone's throw from Piazza Navona.

via Mastro Giorgio 29
+39 06 574 68 00
open 12:30-3 p.m.
and 7:30-11:15 p.m.
feliceatestaccio.it

piazza Fiammetta 10
+39 06 687 57 77
open 12:45-3 p.m.
and 7-11 p.m.; Wed 7-11 p.m.
closed Tue
ristorantefiammetta.it

Forno Campo de' Fiori

Here you'll find Rome's most delicious pizza bianca (pizza with no tomato topping)—crisp, tasty, always hot out of the oven. It's perfect with dressing, but just as scrumptious all by itself. For decades this bakery in Campo de' Fiori has drawn in Romans and tourists alike with its irresistible aromas. Midmorning, lunch, midafternoon, before dinner ... practically all day long the pizza here offers mouth-watering satisfaction. A must for all pizza lovers, this bakery is one of the most alluring stops. So what are you waiting for?

Campo de' Fiori 22
vicolo del Gallo 14
+39 06 688 06 662
open 7:30 a.m.-2:30 p.m.
and 4:45-8 p.m.; closed Sun
fornocampodefiori.com

Giggetto al Portico d'Ottavia

Since 1923 carciofi alla giudia (Jewish-style fried artichokes) and Sora Ines's recipe for cod with tomatoes have been the specialty of this family-run hostaria now in its third generation. Guests are welcomed into the large rooms in traditional trattoria style. And Portico d'Ottavia is an enchanting setting when the weather starts to warm up and dinner can be enjoyed outdoors.

via del Portico d'Ottavia 21
+39 06 686 11 05
open 12:30-3 p.m.
and 7:30-11 p.m.
closed Mon
giggetto.it

GINGER

'GUSTO AL 28

With particular preference for products that are organically grown, this enchanting bistro is especially proud of the fresh and genuine food it serves. The ingredients that make up the special dishes are chosen carefully, and the smoothies and shakes will give you an energy boost at any time of the day.

Under the austere porticoes of Piazza Augusto Imperatore, overlooking the Mausoleum of Augustus, 'Gusto al 28 is like an open lounge, complete with comfortable wicker chairs and French bistro tables. Inside, a huge fireplace hosts a spit where chickens and hens are roasted, along with a grill to cook meat, fish, and vegetables. The grilled squid is unsurpassable, as is the pan pizza.

via Borgognona 43/44
+39 06 699 40 836
open 10 a.m.-1 p.m.
ginger.roma.it

piazza Augusto Imperatore 28
+39 06 681 34 221
open 8 a.m.-midnight
gusto.it

Kosher Bistrot

You can choose to sit down for a light dinner or relax outside surrounded by the historic buildings and comings and goings. The bistro is the 2.0 version of the typical Jewish kosher restaurants in Rome, with a fresh young atmosphere and a delicious menu that is always respectful of tradition. All the ingredients used to make the dishes are given a seal of approval by the local rabbi. And the drinks are great, too.

via di Santa Maria
del Pianto 68/69
+39 06 686 43 98
open 10 a.m.-10 p.m.
closed Sat

La.Vi. Vineria Latteria

On the splendid terrace overlooking Piazza Augusto Imperatore, La.Vi. Vineria Latteria offers made-in-Italy cuisine that serves the best of Rome's traditional food. Start out with carciofi alla giudia (Jewish-style fried artichokes), sweetbreads in sour cream, and beef-tail meatballs. Then try some of the Roman classics: pasta cacio e pepe (pecorino cheese and pepper), all'amatriciana (cured pork cheek, pecorino, tomato), or alla carbonara (bacon and egg), Roman-style tripe, and maialino nero (black pork). The restaurant's motto is "Always remember to smile." This is a great choice for an evening of relaxation and fun, thanks to the long list of drinks that you can sip while listening to the DJ, enveloped by a warm atmosphere.

via Tomacelli 23
+39 06 454 27 760
open 8:30 a.m.-2 a.m.
la-vi.it

Lo Zozzone Pizzeria al taglio

Misticanza

This eatery has been open for almost a century—if you haven't tried it, you can't say you've eaten in Rome! At one time a food store and bakery, today it is the city's most famous pizzeria al taglio (take-out slice of pizza). The pizza bianca (without the tomato topping) is always hot and stuffed with practically anything that's edible. Arranged on the counter are jars of sauce, mushrooms, capers, tomatoes, vegetables . . . and the deli offers an incredible assortment of products. The pizza bianca with mortadella and ricotta is so good, you'll feel like you're in seventh heaven. Sometimes it's closed on Wednesdays—best to check first.

In chic country style, this delightful restaurant describes itself as a "space where the palate is fed." Besides salads and meat, also offered are one-course meals and vegetable delicacies. The goal is to serve genuine food filled with goodness, and all the ingredients are selected from local farms that practice sustainable farming and breeding methods.

via del Teatro Pace 32
+39 06 688 08 575
open 10 a.m.-11 p.m.

via Sicilia 47
+39 06 678 61 15
open 7:30 a.m.- 11:30 p.m.
closed Sun
misticanzaroma.it

NINO DAL 1934

OPEN COLONNA

This restaurant is considered one of Rome's best. Decorated in traditional Italian trattoria style, Nino is a must for people who love a discreet atmosphere, refined service, and kind staff. The menu includes a wide variety of Tuscan dishes, from traditional ribollita (bread and bean soup) to Fiorentina (T-bone steak), from the bruschetta it's famous for to pappardelle with sauce made from game. All the scrumptious desserts here are homemade.

Spectacularly set in the Spazio Serra, at the back of Palazzo delle Esposizioni, is the restaurant run by Chef Antonello Colonna. Tradition and an international spirit characterize the offerings here, renewed each day thanks to ongoing culinary experimentation and a painstaking search for novelty. The inventive and creative cuisine, based on carefully selected ingredients and unexpected pairings, reflects the originality of the venue and the exhibition held in the adjoining museum. Each guest is special in this restaurant. After visiting the show and before sitting down for dinner, do yourself a favor: sip a cocktail on the sunny terrace outside.

via Borgognona 11
+39 06 678 67 52
open 12:30-3 p.m.
and 7:30-11 p.m.
closed Sun
ristorantenino.it

via Milano 9A
+39 06 478 22 641
Tue-Sat 12:30-3:30 p.m.
and 8-11 p.m.
Sun and Mon 12:30-3:30 p.m.
antonellocolonna.it/open

Orazio a Caracalla

At the start of the Passeggiata Archeologica (Archaeological Walk) near the Aurelian Walls is Orazio a Caracalla, a historical Roman restaurant featuring outdoor tables surrounded by a magnificent park overlooking the Baths of Caracalla. Lunch at Orazio's is truly a pleasant break while gazing at one of the most famous open archaeological sites in Rome: the Appian Way. The cuisine here is based on carefully prepared Roman specialties. The grilled meat is a must.

Osteria Bonelli

Reservations are required, best if made a few days before, but don't give up if no one answers at first. Try, try again. This osteria (tavern) is located in the working-class neighborhood of Mandrione, yet it has become a niche venue. The menu includes all the typical dishes of Roman cuisine, and they're not just delicious—the portions are generous and the prices affordable, too. Pasta alla gricia (pasta with cured pork cheek and cheese) and breaded veal slices are a must.

via di Porta Latina 5
+39 06 704 92 401
open 12-3:30 p.m.
and 7-11 p.m.
closed Tue
ristoranteorazio.it

viale dell'Acquedotto
Alessandrino 172/174
+39 329 863 30 77
open 1-2:30 p.m.
and 8-11 p.m.
closed Sun

Ottavio

Il Pagliaccio

The most popular dishes on the menu—raw fish, Catalan-style lobster, pappardelle with astice (small lobster), and fish baked in salt—are a tribute to Mediterranean culture. A warm atmosphere is heightened by the cozy spaces that are never crowded and the hospitality of Adel and Anna and their staff, who provide the magic touch to all the excellent dishes served by this impeccable restaurant. There's also a fine wine list.

The cuisine here, skillfully overseen by three-star chef Anthony Genovese, will amaze with its unexpected pairings: imagination and flavor create new and brilliant harmonies for unusual and unforgettable dishes. Marion Lichtle's wonderful pastries crown the dinner with a selection of excellent dessert.

via di Santa Croce
in Gerusalemme 9
+39 06 702 85 95
open 8-midnight
closed Sun
ottavio.it

via dei Banchi Vecchi 129/A
+39 06 688 09 595
Tue 7-10:30 p.m. Wed-Sat 12-2:30 p.m. and 7-10:30 p.m.
closed Sun and Mon
ristoranteilpagliaccio.com

PANELLA

PASTIFICIO SAN LORENZO

Panella, a bakery that has been around since time immemorial, is now also a café, offering its clientele a tasty break at any time of day. Breakfast is its signature piece, and it's hard to choose between the croissants hot out of the oven, savory crust pastry, pizzas, braided bread, apple turnovers, and all the other desserts made according to recipes that date back to ancient Rome. The specialty here is the cappuccino dei carbonari (the Carbonari were members of a secret revolutionary society in the nineteenth century), a miracle cure on cold days, with a creamy topping whose recipe is a jealously guarded secret.

In the heart of the San Lorenzo neighborhood, at one time solely working class, is an eatery that used to be a pasta factory called Pastificio Cerere, which in the 1980s became the haunt of a group of artists known as the Gruppo San Lorenzo. It still hosts exhibitions, studios, art galleries, and photography schools, as well as the Fondazione Pastificio Cerere for the promotion of contemporary art. Decorated in elegant vintage style, this bistro restaurant is run by Chef Stefano Patelli, who draws inspiration from Roman and Austrian tradition to offer ingredients and flavors that are always à la mode, aiming to satisfy the tastes of the many people who come here from cocktail hour to around midnight.

via Merulana 54
+39 06 487 24 35
Mon-Thur 8 a.m.-11 p.m.
Fri-Sat 8 a.m.-midnight
Sun 8 a.m.-4 p.m.
panellaroma.com

via Tiburtina 196
+ 39 06 972 73 519
open 12:30-3 p.m. and
8-11:30 p.m. Sat 8-11:30 p.m.
closed Sun
pastificiosanlorenzo.com

Pierluigi

Piperno

Since 2014, the kitchen here has been run by the chef and docent Davide Cianetti. Only the best and freshest fish is selected directly from the small fishing boats along the Roman coastline and then cooked as per tradition, but with a modern twist. Besides fish, patrons can choose from meat, vegan, vegetarian, and gluten-free dishes. The gorgeous setting is the sixteenth-century Piazza de' Ricci and its ancient frescoed palazzos, enveloping the tables outside in a magical atmosphere.

Ensconced by the pleasant setting of the piazza, this exclusive restaurant, one of Rome's oldest (established in 1860), is perfect for anyone wanting to try typical Roman food such as carciofi alla giudia (Jewish-style fried artichokes), coda alla vaccinara (beef-tail stew), and pasta all'amatriciana (with cured pork cheek, pecorino, and tomato) or alla carbonara (with bacon and eggs). The warm atmosphere is ideal for hosting large groups in the large frescoed room, cozier evenings in the smaller ones, or special evenings on the quiet piazza when the weather warms up.

piazza de' Ricci 144
+39 06 686 87 17
open 12:30-3 p.m.
and 7:30-11:30 p.m.
pierluigi.it

via Monte de' Cenci 9
+39 06 688 06 629
open 12:45-2:20 p.m.
and 7:45-10:30 p.m.
Sun 12:45-2:20 p.m.; closed Mon
ristorantepiperno.it

Pizzeria Il Leoncino

Pommidoro

One thing that's special about this pizzera is the staff: it's hard to tell the wait staff from the owner, as everyone serves the tables with the same warmth, friendliness and kindness. This is considered one of Rome's top pizzerie, located in the heart of its historical center—in fact, it's in the city's fanciest neighborhood. The rooms are chock-full of rustic décor, and, weather permitting, eating outside on the delightful Via dell'Arancio is ideal. There's always a line, so plan to arrive early.

Located in the picturesque working-class neighborhood of San Lorenzo, and at one time the haunt of intellectuals like Alberto Moravia and Pier Paolo Pasolini, today Pommidoro is a favorite of those artists who, since the 1980s, have set up their studios in what was formerly the Pastificio Cerere (a pasta-making factory), opposite the restaurant. Tripe and beef-tail stew are just two of the traditional dishes that haven't changed over the years. A must for anyone wishing to savor real Roman food.

via del Leoncino 28
+39 06 686 77 57
Mon Tue Thur Fri Sat 1-3 p.m.
and 7 p.m.-midnight
Sun 7 p.m.-midnight
closed Wed

piazza dei Sanniti 46
+39 06 445 26 52
open 12:30-3:30 p.m.
and 7-11 p m.
closed Sun

Primo al Pigneto

Ristorante Ai Piani

One of the most original eateries in the new Roman outskirts, Primo is a hotbed of flavors and temptations for the palate thanks to the endless research of Chef Marco Gallotta. The decor of this restaurant-bistro has been carefully chosen, from the colors of the walls to the large wooden table that takes up the entire third room. The rich wine list varies depending on the season. In the evening the outdoor space is enchanting, while Sunday lunch takes place in the fabulous atmosphere of the neighborhood. Only top-quality ingredients are used here. Try the heavenly spelt linguine produced by the Pastificio Felicetti, served with butter, anchovies, and bread crumbs.

There's something unusual about this restaurant: it's the huge pine tree inside that has become its symbol. The Sardinian cuisine is simple yet well prepared and served, characterized by a wide choice of fresh top-quality fish. The Sardinian fregula (semolina dough) with skate and broccoli is excellent, the spaghetti with telline (wedge shells) second to none. The location—in the heart of the Parioli neighborhood—offers a superb view of Villa Gori Park.

via del Pigneto 46
+39 06 701 38 27
open 7 p.m.-2 a.m.
closed Mon
primoalpigneto.it

via Francesco Denza 35
+39 06 807 97 04
open 1-3 p.m. and 8-11:30 p.m.
closed Sun and Mon
aipiani.it

Ristorante Al Ceppo

A vaguely English, elegant decor with warm wooden paneling, large paintings and mirrors, refined cuisine, and a courteous staff. On the menu are traditional Italian dishes as well as Marches specialties. Whether you choose grilled meat or fish with vegetables Alfredo-style, you can't go wrong here. The wine list is excellent.

Ristorante Atelier Canova Tadolini

This is the place where art enthusiasts will find the magic of workshops from another era while savoring the delicious offerings on the menu. In the nineteenth century, this whole area was teeming with artistic and artisanal botteghe (workshops), the most famous of which was the prestigious sculpture studio run by Antonio Canova and his assistant Adamo Tadolini. Today at this sophisticated café-restaurant, guests can enjoy a special lunch amid the marbles and preparatory plaster models that have survived from Canova's bottega.

via Panama 2
+39 06 855 13 79
open 12:30-3 p.m.
and 7:30-11 p.m.
Mon 7:30-11 p.m.
ristorantealceppo.it

via del Babuino 150/A
+39 06 321 10 702
open 8 a.m.-midnight
canovatadolini.com

Ristorante Consolini

The atmosphere is enchanting in this elegant four-level restaurant that offers a breathtaking view from its two balconies in the Testaccio neighborhood, at the foot of Aventine Hill. The restaurant serves typical Roman dishes, starting with the wonderful pasta with cacio e pepe (pecorino cheese and pepper)—a favorite of Federico Fellini, who was a regular here—matched with perfect wines from the well-stocked cellar. This is the ideal place for a romantic meal.

via Marmorata 28
+39 06 573 00 148
open 12-3 p.m.
and 7:30 p.m.-midnight
closed Mon
ristoranteconsolini.it

Ristoro degli Angeli

A welcoming atmosphere and family recipes passed down from generation to generation, as well as those supplied by neighborhood residents, are what characterize this unusual eatery that's certain to become one of your secret destinations in Rome. The owner makes the fruit compotes that go with an assortment of cheeses. And don't forget to try the cheese and pepper bread, also made by the owner. It's worth a trip, perhaps after admiring the unique architecture of the social housing built in the 1920s in the Garbatella neighborhood, modeled after English garden cities.

via Luigi Orlando 2
+39 06 514 36 020
open 12:30-2:30 p.m.
and 7:30-11:30 p.m.
closed Sun
ristorodegliangeli.it

Roscioli

La Rosetta

Eating while sitting at the counters of this delicatessen is an unusual, characteristic, and amusing experience. This is so not just because of the way the tables are arranged, but because of the delicious menu, whose superb cold cuts, famous in Rome, and selection of Italian and French cheeses go perfectly with Roman cuisine. Not to mention the olive oil, which is truly special and guarantees dressings that are both genuine and high quality.

Close to the Pantheon and open since 1966, La Rosetta is the place to eat fish in Rome. Chef Massimo Riccioli satisfies even the most demanding palates with dishes that are characterized by quality and the fragrance of the flavors. An oyster bar (open daily from 12 a.m. to 7 p.m.) offers a low-cost menu for top-quality food, with a selection of only the finest oysters. The list of French Champagnes is so refined that the French embassy crowned Chef Riccioli a Chevalier de l'Ordre des Coteaux de Champagne.

via dei Giubbonari 21
+39 06 687 52 87
open 12:30-4 p.m.
and 7 p.m.-midnight
closed Sun
salumeriaroscioli.com

via della Rosetta 8/9
+39 06 686 10 02
open 12-11 p.m.
larosettaristorante.it

SAID

IL SANLORENZO

What was once a chocolate factory in 1923 is now a shrine for cocoa enthusiasts, offering an impressive choice of different chocolate varieties as well as a library with a vast selection of publications on this tasty subject. The restaurant, which is open for lunch and dinner, offers many traditional Roman dishes renewed with élan and originality, as well as exquisite desserts, of course.

Fish is brought here each day thanks to the collaboration that began in 2007 with the cooperative of Ponza fishermen. Vongole veraci (real baby clams) from Sabaudia appear on a menu that changes all the time while still maintaining fundamental dishes: its version of raw fish; spelt spaghetti with Ponza anchovies, bread crumbs, and peppers baked in cinders; and, when in season, spaghetti with ricci (sea urchins). The decor is elegant and perfect for a tête-à-tête or, why not, something special!

via Tiburtina 135
+39 06 446 92 04
Mon 7:30 p.m.-12:30 a.m.
Tue-Thur 10 a.m.-12:30 a.m.
Fri-Sat 10 a.m.-1:30 a.m.
Sun 10 a.m.-midnight;
said.it

via dei Chiavari 4/5
+39 06 686 50 97
Mon and Sat 7:30-11:45 p.m.
Tue Wed Thur Fri 12:45-2:45 p.m.
and 7:30-11:45 p.m.; closed Sun
ilsanlorenzo.it

SANTA LUCIA

LA SANTERIA

This charming restaurant in a small square right behind Piazza Navona is truly enchanting. A favorite place for artists and celebrities from the stage and set, Santa Lucia will welcome you to its magical scenario, especially if you manage to get a table in the lovely garden when the weather is warm. The typical Neapolitan cuisine is supervised by chefs of international standing who constantly renew the offerings. A simple but refined menu and a competent, courteous staff are the perfect "ingredients" for a stylish culinary experience.

Right in the heart of the Pigneto, on the outskirts of Rome, the Santeria Pizzicheria-Bistro has in recent years become one of the city's trendiest haunts. It's the ideal place for a before-dinner drink at the end of the workday or a glass of wine at night, accompanied by a scarpetta, pita bread stuffed with a surprising mix of only the highest-quality ingredients. The choice of wines is excellent and changes all the time.

largo Febo 12
+39 06 688 02 427
open 12-3 p.m.
and 7-11 p.m.
closed Tue
santaluciaristorante.it

via del Pigneto 211
+39 06 648 01 606
open 6:30 p.m.-1:30 a.m.

SETTIMIO AL PELLEGRINO

SETTIMIO ALL'ARANCIO

Located at the end of Via del Pellegrino is this tranquil restaurant, which from the outside might look like it's closed but is probably crowded inside, with Romans especially. You'll have to ring the doorbell, as if you were visiting a friend, to be let in. The atmosphere is welcoming and familiar, like being at home . . . and probably because it's so much like home, the service isn't always perfect. But the delicious menu makes up for it. The cuisine is traditional, simple, and reassuring: Signora Teresa's handmade tagliatelle is a treat, as are the stracciatella (egg drop soup), boiled meats, and meatballs. The ice cream is among the finest in all of Rome.

Right behind Piazza San Lorenzo in Lucina, on a quiet side street with no traffic and none of the hustle and bustle of shops, is Settimio all'Arancio. Here you'll be overcome by the delightful owners as well as by the rich menu (which includes excellent meat dishes and traditional, carefully prepared fish recipes) that turn a lunch break into a delightful experience. Outdoor tables are heated so that customers can enjoy the view even when temperatures fall. The list of leading wines, both Italian and French, is excellent, featuring over 400 labels.

via del Pellegrino 117
+39 06 688 01 978
open 12-3:30 p.m.
and 7 p.m.-midnight
closed Sun

via dell'Arancio 50
+39 06 687 61 19
open 12-4 p.m.
and 7 p.m.-midnight
closed Sun
settimioallarancio.it

IL SORPASSO

LA TAVERNA DEGLI AMICI

"Genuine products at reasonable prices" is the philosophy of this restaurant-bistro-wine cellar that offers a wide choice of cold cuts and cheeses, organized by region, that's truly special. The cold cuts are to die for, produced by a small company that uses only naturally fed and bred animals.

This unique rustic trattoria with wooden ceiling beams is almost hidden within the maze of tiny streets behind Piazza Venezia. Customers are welcomed into a familiar atmosphere where traditional Roman dishes are served. Weather permitting, eating outside surrounded by this delightful piazza is an unforgettable experience.

via Properzio 31/33
+39 06 890 24 554
open 7:30 a.m.-1 p.m.
Sat 9 a.m.-1 a.m.
closed Sun
sorpasso.info

piazza Margana 37
+39 06 699 20 637
open 12-11 p.m.
closed Mon
latavernadegliamici.net

La Taverna del Ghetto

Tempio di Iside, Cottura 0°

At the Taverna del Ghetto, Jewish kosher cuisine is perfectly combined with typical Roman dishes, and their close connection, which goes way back in time, is accentuated by the special, characteristic dishes that draw from the finest tradition. As for the menu, the kashrut, or Jewish dietary laws in the Torah, is rigorously followed, such as the distinction between permitted and forbidden foods and the separation between meat and dairy.

This is the shrine of "fresh fish" enthusiasts, whether raw or cooked. Fish appetizers (raw, cold, warm), delicious first courses, and original second courses vaunt basic ingredients of absolute quality, personally chosen by the chef to guarantee customers only the best every time. Each day the right selection is made to combine just the right colors, flavors, and emotions. The Tempio often hosts other renowned chefs, like Nobuyuki Matsuhisa, known simply as Nobu. The wine list is long and special. Reservations are advised.

via del Portico d'Ottavia 8
+39 06 688 09 771
Sun-Thur 12-11 p.m.
Fri 12-3 p.m. Sat 6-11 p.m.
latavernadelghetto.com

via Labicana 50
corner of via Pietro Verri
+39 06 700 47 41
open 12:30-3 p.m.
and 7-11:30 p.m. closed Sun
isideristorante.it

THE CORNER RESTAURANT

This splendid restaurant at the foot of Aventine Hill boasts a five-star chef, Marco Martini, and is characterized by large windows that allow the spacious rooms to converse with the evocative hanging garden. The atmosphere is refined, as is the menu, which varies according to the seasons, in a delicate balance between "eyes, stomach, and head," as the chef likes to say, i.e. appearance, traditional flavors, and innovation, the fruit of careful exploration.

viale Aventino 121
+39 06 455 97 350
open 12:30-3 p.m.
and 7:30-11 p.m.
closed Sun
thecornerrome.com/restaurant

TIEPOLO - BISTROT BOTTIGLIERIA

This informal and colorful eatery is for people who want to relax while enjoying a one-course meal and discovering new food combinations in a young, fresh, and sparkling atmosphere. It is truly a pleasure, and the dishes are both unique and delicious. Be sure to try the scamorza (cheese) with gorgonzola and walnuts, a delightful surprise for cheese lovers.

via Giovanni Battista Tiepolo 3
+39 06 322 74 49
open 1-3 p.m.
and 5:30 p.m.-midnight

TRATTORIA AL MORO

"If you miss the golden days, go to the Moro," they say in Rome . . . Behind the Trevi Fountain is this haven of Roman cuisine, an absolute must for anyone who wishes to get a feel for the flavors, colors, and aromas of local tradition. And Roman-ness is everywhere here, from the typical dishes to the kindness of the staff, from the retro decor to the glory of this historic venue. Spaghetti alla Moro, pasta alla carbonara (with bacon and eggs) that you'll never forget, is a must here.

vicolo delle Bollette 13
+39 06 678 34 95
open 1-3:30 p.m.
and 8-11:30 p.m.
closed Sun
ristorantealmororoma.com

TRATTORIA AL POMPIERE

The rather unusual name of this restaurant comes from the owner's nickname. Pompiere means "fireman" in Italian, and that's the kind of person who was needed to put out the fire that scalded the mouths of the customers after tasting one of the kitchen's famous spicy dishes: penne all'arrabbiata (tomato and chili pepper). For those who are keen on trying traditional Roman cuisine, the pecorara is a must, a mixture of fried foods including abbacchio (lamb) cutlets, artichokes, calf's brain, and ricotta.

via di Santa Maria
de' Calderari 38
+39 06 686 83 77
open 12:30-3 p.m.
and 7:30-11 p.m. closed Sun
alpompiereroma.com

TRATTORIA DAL CAVALIER GINO

TREEBAR

In this small old-fashioned trattoria, whose walls are hung with paintings, diners will find all the genuineness of traditional Roman cuisine: generous servings abundantly dressed, tables close together, pleasant and lively service—all will take you back in time. Politicians and people in the entertainment world are regulars because this is where you can eat real food, from those who know exactly how to make it.

The location is truly unique: immersed in the greenery of the gardens of Piazza Manila is a modern wooden lodge with minimal architectural lines but that has something warm about it, too. The wine and cocktail list is long and carefully structured, as are the smoothies and shakes. The rich menu includes a mouth-watering selection of cold cuts and cheeses.

vicolo Rosini 4
+39 06 687 34 34
open 1-2:30 p.m.
and 8-10:30 p.m.
closed Sun

via Flaminia 226
+39 06 326 52 754
Tue-Sun 12:30-3:30 p.m.
and 6:30 p.m.-1:30 a.m.
Mon 6:30 p.m.-1:30 a.m.
treebar.it

URBANA 47

LA ZANZARA

This was the first restaurant in Rome to embrace the "zero kilometer" philosophy—that is, to use only locally grown and produced ingredients. Idea for lunch, dinner, or even a snack, it serves specialties from the Lazio region but with a new twist, which vary depending on the season. The decor is delightful: tables, sofas, and chairs from the 1970s, and lots of vintage. If you see something you like, you can even buy it!

Characterized by large glass window panes and big rooms, this bistro with an international air is in the heart of the Prati neighborhood. It is always crowded thanks to the great choice of dishes, excellent cocktails, and the fact that you can go there "All Day Long," from breakfast to dinner. Weather permitting, eating outdoors at the small but dainty tables is a lovely experience.

via Urbana 47
+39 06 478 84 006
open 8:30 a.m.-midnight
urbana47.it

via Crescenzio 84
+39 06 683 92 227
open 8 a.m.-2 a.m.
lazanzararoma.com

Zoc Trattoria

Zuma

Located on a hidden side street right in the historical center of Rome, behind the Lungotevere dei Vallati, Zoc is a loft with a garden where local produce is filled with spices from distant lands and a mixture of flavors. The vintage decor is unique and creates just the right atmosphere. Listed on a large primary-school blackboard are the day's specials, which always include both traditional and new offerings.

The refined Zuma brand has been successful ever since it first opened in London in 2002, and now it can also be enjoyed at Palazzo FENDI in Rome. The exclusive decor, designed by Muramatsu Noriyoshi, accentuates the energy of the venue for a haute cuisine experience inspired by the informal style of the izakaya (gastropub), which includes a sushi counter and robata grilling right before your eyes. We suggest rare tuna with daikon, chili pepper and ponzu, the selection of marinated fish, avocado, and gobo on sushi rice, the bed of spicy beef, the black cod marinated in miso, the giant shrimp with yuku. For dessert, the chawan mushi with dried fruit is superb. It's best to book well in advance.

via delle Zoccolette 22
+39 06 681 92 515
open 8 a.m.-4 p.m. and
6 p.m.-midnight; Sat and Sun 9:30
a.m.-4 p.m. and 6 p.m.-midnight
zoc22.it

Palazzo FENDI
Via della Fontanella di Borghese 48
+39 06 992 66 622
open 12-3 p.m. and 7-11:30 p.m.
closed Mon
zumarestaurant.com

FROM DUSK TILL DAWN

Akab Club

Alibi Club

Located in the characteristic Testaccio neighborhood, in what used to be a carpenter's workshop, the Akab Club organizes evenings with live music played by bands both famous and less so. Situated on two levels, with a small garden at the entrance and the typical neon lights, the Akab is a point of reference for Roman clubbers. It's also a place that doesn't shy away from the latest trends in music, offering, for example, acid jazz nights, L-ektrica evenings, and milkshake parties. The calendar of events varies, so it's best to contact the club for information.

Located on three levels, the Alibi Club started out as a gay club, but over the years it has become less exclusive and now welcomes a wide range of customers. Modeled after the 1980s New York club scene, it has large dark spaces lit by strobe lights, plus a huge terrace. Concerts are held and movies are screened, which are often "gay and friendly." Information and opening times are available on its website.

via di Monte Testaccio 69
+39 06 572 50 585
Thur, Fri and Sat
midnight-5 a.m.
akabclub.com

via di Monte Testaccio 40
+39 574 34 48
Fri and Sat 11:30 p.m.-5 a.m.
lalibi.it

Art Cafè

This is believed by many to be the city's most elegant disco thanks to its splendid location, the Villa Borghese. For patrons—members of the national and international jet set—it's the best place to go to have fun and dance until the wee hours; it's also the venue for exclusive fashion and cinema events. Opening hours depend on the evening, so contact the club before arriving.

Cantina Ripagrande

This club gets its name from the Ripa Grande, the ancient river port on the Tiber where wares were once traded. This cozy, well-stocked wine cellar offers an excellent selection of wines and tasty dishes, prepared and presented with great skill. The background music is pleasant, and the staff is very hospitable. Highly recommended for before and after dinner.

viale del Galoppatoio 33
+39 348 357 88 15
Fri and Sat 11 p.m.-5 a.m.
art-cafe.it

via di San Francesco a Ripa 73
+39 06 645 47 62 37
open 12:30 p.m.-2 a.m.
closed Sun

Duke's

Enoteca Buccone

Considered one of the best cafés in the city, Duke's serves special lighter cocktails that are full of surprises in terms of taste, consistency, and fragrance. The specialty is the "Cocktail Light," half alcohol and half pure organic aloe vera juice.

Originally the coach house of the marquesses Cavalcabò, the building later became a tavern and, since 1969, has been one of Rome's finest wine cellars, a stone's throw from Piazza del Popolo. It was the first wine cellar in Rome to serve high quality wines by the glass. A must for both expert oenologists and people who just love good wine.

viale Parioli 200
+39 06 806 62 455
open 7 p.m.-2 a.m.
closed Sun and Mon
dukes.it

via di Ripetta 19/20
+39 06 361 21 54
Sun 11 a.m.-7 p.m., Mon-Thur
9 a.m.-8:30 p.m.
Fri and Sat 9 a.m.-11:30 p.m.
www.enotecabuccone.com

ENOTECA CAVOUR

ENOTECA COSTANTINI

This wine cellar offers a cozy environment, characterized by wood paneling, and more than 1,000 labels of excellent wines, especially Italian ones, as well as a tasty menu of gastronomic specialties. The retro style and quick, discreet service make it the ideal place for a business date or a night on the town with friends.

The most enchanting of the city's wine cellars, overlooking Piazza Cavour, the Costantini features elegant decorations in Italian Liberty style at the entrance. Once inside, patrons will be surprised to learn that they can enter the cellar. With over 4,000 labels and almost 1,000 different spirits, this is truly a shrine for wine enthusiasts and a must for curiosity seekers.

via Cavour 313
+39 06 678 54 96
open 12:30-2:45 p.m.
and 7:30 p.m.-12:30 a.m.
cavour313.it

piazza Cavour 16
+39 06 320 35 75
Tue-Sat 9 a.m.-1 p.m. and
4:30-8 p.m. Mon 4:30-8 p.m.
closed Sun
pierocostantini.it

ENOTECA DEL FRATE

ENOTECA FERRARA

Over 3,000 labels of fine wines are stocked in this historical wine cellar in the heart of the Prati neighborhood, which has been a classic venue for wine lovers since 1922. Much attention is paid to pairing wines and cheeses, and painstaking efforts are made to heighten the authenticity of flavors and aromas. Let the kind and competent staff guide you in your discovery of good food and good drinking.

In the heart of the Trastevere neighborhood, right in the building where the ancient convent of Sant'Eufemia used to be, the Enoteca Ferrara is a quiet corner in which to sip a good glass of wine, choosing from among the more than 1,600 different labels available. Special appetizers are served to go with each drink. This is the perfect place to relax after roaming around the maze of side streets in this part of the city.

via degli Scipioni 118/122
+39 06 321 19 18
open 9 a.m.-1:30 p.m. and 4-8 p.m.; wine bar 12:30-3 and 6:30 p.m.-1 a.m. closed Sun
enotecadelfrate.it

piazza Trilussa 41
+39 06 583 33 920
open 6 p.m.-2 a.m.
enotecaferrara.it

Enoteca Il Goccetto

Located in the historical Palazzetto del Vescovo di Cervia, on Via dei Banchi Vecchi, is a wine cellar whose patrons are habitués and wine lovers in general; its shelves rising all the way up to the ceiling are filled with bottles produced by only the finest winemakers. Arranged on the counter is a great variety of excellent cheeses and cold cuts, accompanied by fresh bread from Lariano. The retro decor and dim lighting create a cozy, calm atmosphere.

Goa Club

This historical temple of house music in Rome was founded by the DJ producer Giancarlo Battafarano, and over the years it has hosted the best musicians and DJs from Italy and abroad. The huge dance floor has an island bar in the center, specially designed to serve customers as efficiently as possible. There's a second bar in a more private area behind the console. Be sure to check what's on and the opening times before you go.

via dei Banchi Vecchi 14
+39 06 686 42 68
Tue-Sat 11:30 a.m.-2:30 p.m.
and 6:30 p.m.-midnight
Mon 6:30 p.m.-midnight closed Sun
ilgoccetto.com

via di Libetta 13
+39 06 574 82 77
Mon, Wed, Thur, Fri,
and Sun 24 hours a day
closed Tue and Sat
goaclub.com

Lola

Piper Club

Thanks to the experience of Armando Bomba, one of the most famous bartenders in Rome, the Lola cocktail bar offers cleverly made drinks with the addition of "secret" ingredients for an original, delicious touch. The location inside an ancient villa with a garden is charming.

This historic Roman disco, described in the Enciclopedia Treccani as the "symbol of beat and 'yé yé' music in Italy," has been a place for musical experiments and influences since February 17, 1965. The most renowned artists have performed here, and it's where Patty Pravo became famous. The Piper often hosts live performances, and for the past half century it has preserved its title as the temple of pop music. The acoustics are considered the best in Rome, and taking turns at the console are musicians and DJs of all kinds from around the world. The room is divided into several spaces, and there's a terrace as well as more private areas. The program varies. Check opening times.

via Flaminia 305
+39 06 321 92 79
Tue-Sun 7 a.m.-2 a.m.
Mon 7 a.m.-4 p.m.
lolaroma.it

via Tagliamento 9
+39 06 855 53 98
Fri and Sat 11 p.m.-5 a.m.
piperclub.it

Salotto 42

The atmosphere here is elegant and international, as are the customers. Located opposite the Temple of Hadrian, for the past decade Salotto 42 has been a rendezvous in the historical center of the capital, the perfect place to sip a great drink while leafing through a magazine or art catalogue. It's also ideal for anyone wanting to spend a quiet evening with friends in the lovely Piazza di Pietra.

piazza di Pietra 42
+39 06 678 58 04
open 10 a.m.-2 a.m.
salotto42.space.it

Settembrini Caffé

Whether you're calling it a day or just getting the evening started, a drink at Settembrini's is always a pleasure. Seating is both inside, where the atmosphere is more intimate, or outside in the heart of the Prati neighborhood. This is the place where lots of names from the entertainment world love to spend their spare time. The cocktails are always different and imaginative, as are the appetizers, which range from traditional Roman pizza stuffed with mortadella to delicious sushi, sometimes served Italian-style.

via Luigi Settembrini 19/27
+39 06 976 10 325
open 7 a.m.-1:30 a.m.
Sun 8 a.m.-1:30 a.m.
viasettembrini.com

Spazio Novecento

The Jerry Thomas Speakeasy Project

The entrance to this club in the EUR area of Rome is imposing, and the two stories are connected by a large marble staircase. A perfect example of Italian Rationalist style, the terrace has large travertine columns that frame the view of Piazza dell'Obelisco, as well as roomy interiors with very high ceilings. Despite the size of the place, the sound quality is excellent. The rich calendar of events, as well as opening times, should always be checked online or by phone.

Everyone knows that speakeasies were illicit establishments that sold alcoholic beverages during the Prohibition era in the United States, and this mysterious club, inspired by the Roaring Twenties, requires customers to say a password (you'll get yours when you call to make a reservation) in order to enter. The keen bartenders will suggest which of the fabulous drinks to order, but remember, Jerry Thomas has certain rules that everyone must follow. Check the website to find out what they are.

piazza Guglielmo Marconi 26/B
+39 06 542 21 107
Mon-Fri 10 a.m.-6 p.m.
closed Sat and Sun
spazionovecento.it

vicolo Cellini 30
+39 370 114 62 87
Tue-Sat 1 p.m.-4 a.m.
closed Sun and Mon
thejerrythomasproject.it

Vicious Club

The atmosphere is dark, the look is total black, and the indie electronic music is predominant in this famous Roman nightclub. Actors, artists, musicians, politicians, ordinary people, and eccentrics all meet in this underground venue that knows exactly how to welcome its multifarious clientele. You have to be on a list to get in. Call to make a reservation and get information on events and opening times.

via Achille Grandi 7/a
+ 39 06 706 14 349
Mon-Thur 10 p.m.-4 a.m.
Fri-Sun 10 p.m.-6 a.m.
viciousclub.com

Zuma Bar Lounge & Roof Top

Enjoy the breathtaking view of the historic city center from the terrace of this new lounge on the fifth floor of the Palazzo FENDI, where guests can have a drink accompanied by Zuma's unmistakable delicacies, like finely sliced sea urchin, green pepper delight, ponzu and garlic in brine, and angler tempura with yozu, crisp calamari, green chili, and lime. The cocktail master par excellence is Stefano d'Ippolito, who came here after working in London. Suggestions are a Negroni aged in a terracotta amphora, a new-fangled Spritz, Rubabu, Bellini Zuma, and Biwa No Choiu, sake made exclusively for Zuma.

Palazzo FENDI
via della Fontanella di Borghese 48
+39 06 992 66 622
open 6-11 p.m.
zumarestaurant.com

BODY AND SOUL

- acquaMadre
- Alta Care Beauty
- Silvano Rossi the Barber
- Fabrizio Narducci
  for Gili Beauty & spa

- Kami Spa
- Luxury Gym Margutta
- Spa La Mer
- Wonderfool

SALUS
PER AQUAM

alus per aquam and *sanitas per aquam* are Latin expressions that, when abbreviated, become spa, meaning "health via water." The words refer to the ancient Roman baths, those public buildings that were used to cure the body and the spirit, as well as the places where people could meet, socialize, and do business. They are the precursors of today's health spas, which offer wellness and relaxation in the company of others. After a day spent in Rome's museums, markets, and shops, why not bask in the healthy steam of a spa or perhaps indulge in a haircut at Silvano's, the barber known as the "artist of the razor." You're guaranteed a leap back into history.

acquaMadre

Tepidarium, calidarium, frigidarium: a steam bath cleans out toxins, improves circulation and breathing, stimulates the body's defenses, relaxes, mitigates rheumatic pain, and staves off anxiety and stress. Inspired by the hammam of Greco-Roman baths, acquaMadre offers you a relaxing massage after you finish bathing.

via di Sant'Ambrogio 17
+39 06 686 42 72
appointments can be booked
closed Mon
acquamadre.it

Alta Care Beauty

The ideal place for relaxation after a hard day's shopping among Rome's busy streets, this five-story building offers a breathtaking view of Piazza di Spagna and the magnificent Spanish Steps. The spa guarantees a five-star sensory experience through exclusive beauty and wellness treatments. The regenerating effects will stay with you for the rest of the day, reenergizing you for more Italian adventures.

piazza di Spagna 6
+39 06 693 80 852
appointments can be booked
altacare.com

Silvano Rossi the Barber

It is as though time stands still in this historical barber's shop on the corner of Via dell'Orso and Via dei Pianellari. The decor is original, from the sign carved in marble and the comfortable leather chairs to the tools of the trade. Silvano Rossi uses his skills to style the hair of stars in the entertainment world, artists, and ordinary people, too. There are many who have heard about him and can't wait to put themselves in the hands of this renowned master barber.

via dei Pianellari 31
+39 06 686 98 81
Tue-Sat 8 a.m.-6 p.m.
closed Sun and Mon

Fabrizio Narducci for Gili Beauty & Spa

For almost two decades his name has been synonymous with luxury hairdressing. An absolute star, today Fabrizio Narducci works freelance in the Rossano Ferretti salon at Hotel Hassler and opens the doors of his salon to customers from around the world, offering unique advice about color, cut, and style. Thanks to his long-standing collaboration with photographers, filmmakers, and television professionals, Narducci has opened an agency that deals with improving the image of those appearing in movies or on TV. Trust him, you'll be sure to enjoy his "special effects."

piazza Trinità dei Monti 6
+39 346 09 89 549
appointments can be booked
fabrizionarducci.com

Kami Spa

Luxury Gym Margutta

Available here is all the wisdom of the Far East to help shed one's everyday stress, experience the centuries-old knowledge of Tibet, Burma, Japan, Thailand, India, Indonesia, and China, and try every possible Asian massage technique. The Buddhist staff guarantees a unique sensory experience, with a variety of fabulous therapies to restore one's energy.

Give yourself the gift of 55 minutes with a personal trainer whose only goal is to help you achieve the health, beauty, wellness, and shape you long for. In the exclusive and reserved atmosphere you'll find fabulous "motivators" capable of turning you into an athlete in no time at all. Luxury Gym's trainers are highly qualified in sports, diet, and myriad techniques, including Personal Kinesis, CrossFit, Pilates, and Circuit Training.

via degli Avignonesi 11/12
+39 06 420 10 039
open 10 a.m.-10 p.m.
kamispa.com

via Margutta 54
+39 06 976 11 635
open 8 a.m.-8 p.m.
Sat 8 a.m.-6 p.m.
closed Sun
marguttaluxurygym.com

Spa La Mer

Wonderfool

Luxury rooms for massages, a tub for thalassotherapy, a sauna, and a Turkish bath will immerse you in the magic of this spa, inside the Hotel Aldrovandi Villa Borghese, where you can also purchase La Mer products, ideal for facial and body care.

Guaranteed by the quality of the HUR laboratories in Florence, the Wonderfool spa is a complete wellness center. Here, patrons can escape from the stressful pace of everyday life and enjoy a complete range of massages, as well as cosmetic, anti-aging, and relaxation treatments. The spa also includes a hair salon and a concept store, where customers can choose among the products selected with passion that come from all around the world.

via Ulisse Aldrovandi 15
+39 06 322 39 93
appointments can be booked
aldrovandi.com

via dei Banchi Nuovi 39
+39 06 688 92 315
open Tue-Sat 9:30 a.m.-8 p.m.
May-Sep also Mon 9:30 a.m.-8 p.m.
Oct-Apr also Sun 1-8 p.m.
wonderfool.it

YOUR OWN PERSONAL ROME

Notes

NOTES

NOTES

NOTES

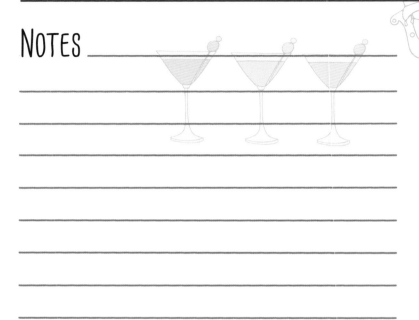

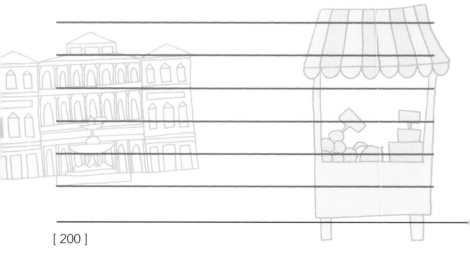

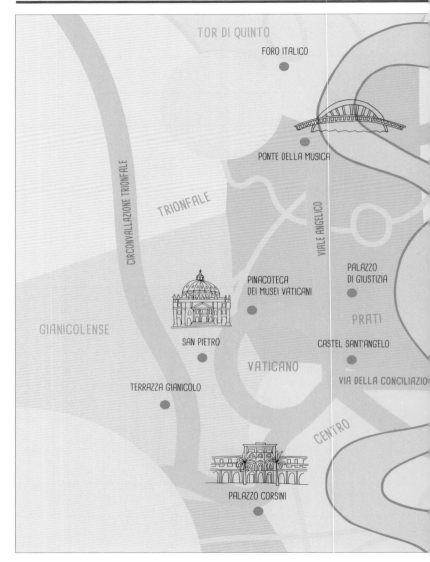

TOR DI QUINTO

FORO ITALICO

PONTE DELLA MUSICA

CIRCONVALLAZIONE TRIONFALE

TRIONFALE

VIALE ANGELICO

PINACOTECA
DEI MUSEI VATICANI

PALAZZO
DI GIUSTIZIA

PRATI

GIANICOLENSE

SAN PIETRO

CASTEL SANT'ANGELO

VATICANO

VIA DELLA CONCILIAZIO

TERRAZZA GIANICOLO

CENTRO

PALAZZO CORSINI

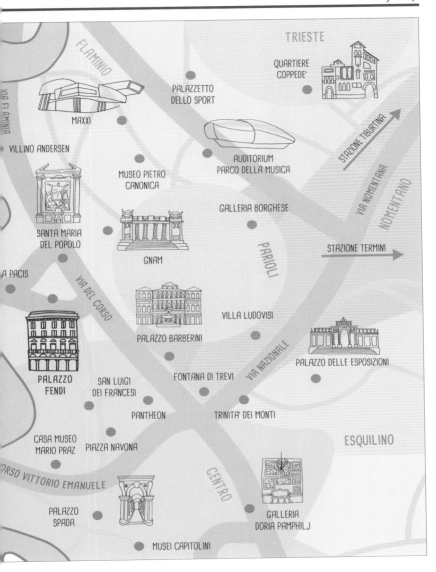

FLAMINIO

TRIESTE

QUARTIERE
COPPEDE'

PALAZZETTO
DELLO SPORT

VIA FLAMINIA

MAXXI

VILLINO ANDERSEN

STAZIONE TIBURTINA

AUDITORIUM
PARCO DELLA MUSICA

MUSEO PIETRO
CANONICA

VIA NOMENTANA

NOMENTANO

GALLERIA BORGHESE

SANTA MARIA
DEL POPOLO

PARIOLI

GNAM

STAZIONE TERMINI

A PACIS

VIA DEL CORSO

PALAZZO BARBERINI

VILLA LUDOVISI

PALAZZO
FENDI

SAN LUIGI
DEI FRANCESI

FONTANA DI TREVI

VIA NAZIONALE

PALAZZO DELLE ESPOSIZIONI

PANTHEON

TRINITA' DEI MONTI

CASA MUSEO
MARIO PRAZ

PIAZZA NAVONA

ESQUILINO

ORSO VITTORIO EMANUELE

CENTRO

PALAZZO
SPADA

GALLERIA
DORIA PAMPHILJ

MUSEI CAPITOLINI

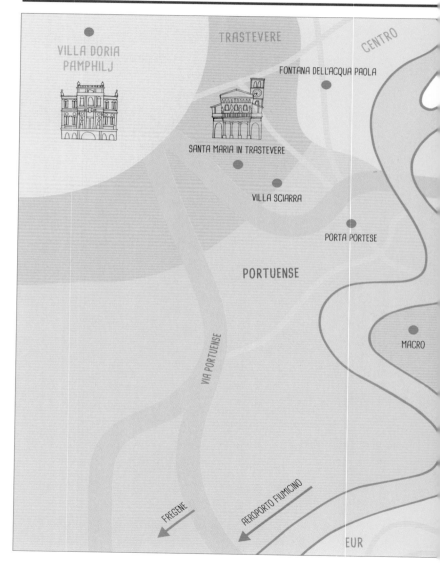

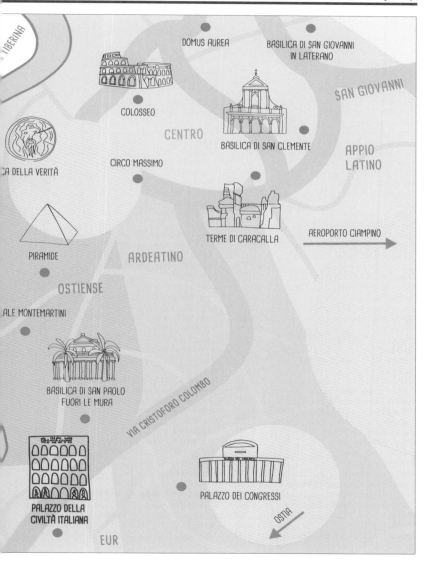

IBERINA

DOMUS AUREA

BASILICA DI SAN GIOVANNI
IN LATERANO

SAN GIOVANNI

COLOSSEO

CENTRO

BASILICA DI SAN CLEMENTE

APPIO
LATINO

CA DELLA VERITÀ

CIRCO MASSIMO

TERME DI CARACALLA

AEROPORTO CIAMPINO

PIRAMIDE

ARDEATINO

OSTIENSE

ALE MONTEMARTINI

BASILICA DI SAN PAOLO
FUORI LE MURA

VIA CRISTOFORO COLOMBO

PALAZZO DEI CONGRESSI

PALAZZO DELLA
CIVILTÀ ITALIANA

OSTIA

EUR

[Index]

Art and Parks

Restaurants, Shopping, and More Fun